RANK

HYPOCRISIES

SAGE SWIFTS

In 1976 SAGE published a series of short 'university papers', which led to the publication of the QASS series (or the 'little green books' as they became known to researchers). Almost 40 years since the release of the first 'little green book', SAGE is delighted to offer a new series of swift, short and topical pieces in the ever-growing digital environment.

SAGE *Swifts* offer authors a new channel for academic research with the freedom to deliver work outside the conventional length of journal articles. The series aims to give authors speedy access to academic audiences through digital first publication, space to explore ideas thoroughly, yet at a length which can be readily digested, and the quality stamp and reassurance of peer-review.

RANK

HYPOCRISIES

THE INSULT OF THE REF

DEREK SAYER

SAGE SWIFTS

Los Angeles | London | New Delhi
Singapore | Washington DC

Los Angeles | London | New Delhi
Singapore | Washington DC

SAGE Publications Ltd
1 Oliver's Yard
55 City Road
London EC1Y 1SP

SAGE Publications Inc.
2455 Teller Road
Thousand Oaks, California 91320

SAGE Publications India Pvt Ltd
B 1/I 1 Mohan Cooperative Industrial Area
Mathura Road
New Delhi 110 044

SAGE Publications Asia-Pacific Pte Ltd
3 Church Street
#10-04 Samsung Hub
Singapore 049483

Editor: Chris Rojek
Assistant editor: Gemma Shield
Production editor: Vanessa Harwood
Marketing manager: Michael Ainsley
Cover design: Jen Crisp
Typeset by: C&M Digitals (P) Ltd, Chennai, India
Printed and bound by CPI Group (UK) Ltd,
Croydon, CR0 4YY (for Anthony Rowe)

Professor Derek Sayer was employed by Lancaster University at the time this book was written; the University did not authorize, and was otherwise unaware of, Professor Sayer's work on this publication. The views and opinions expressed in this publication are those of the author and do not represent those of, and should not in any way be attributed to, the University.

Library of Congress Control Number: 2014945632

British Library Cataloguing in Publication data

A catalogue record for this book is available from the British Library

MIX
Paper from
responsible sources
FSC® C013604

ISBN 978-1-4739-0656-3
eISBN 978-1-4739-1064-5

At SAGE we take sustainability seriously. We print most of our products in the UK. These are produced using FSC papers and boards. We undertake an annual audit on materials used to ensure that we monitor our sustainability in what we are doing. When we print overseas, we ensure that sustainable papers are used, as measured by the Egmont grading system.

Derek Sayer's book is essential reading for all university researchers and research policy makers. It discusses the waste, biases and pointlessness of Britain's Research Excellence Framework (REF), and its misuse by universities. The book is highly readable, astute, sharply analytical and very intelligent. It paints a devastating portrait of a scheme that is useless for advancing research and that does no better job at ranking research performance than do the global indexes but does so for a huge cost in time, money, duplication, and irritation. Anyone interested in research ranking, assessment, and the contemporary condition of the universities should read this book.
Peter Murphy, Professor of Arts and Society, James Cook University

Sayer makes a compelling argument that the Research Excellence Framework is not only expensive and divisive, but is also deeply flawed as an evaluation exercise. *Rank Hypocrisies* is a rigorous and scholarly evaluation of the REF, yet written in a lively and engaging style that makes it highly readable.
Dorothy Bishop, University of Oxford

Many academics across the world have come to see the REF – and its RAE predecessor – as an arrogant attempt to raise national research standards that has resulted in a variety of self-inflicted wounds to UK higher education. Derek Sayer is the Thucydides of this situation. A former head of the Lancaster history department, he fell on his sword trying to deal with a university that behaved in an increasingly irrational manner as it tried to game a system that is fundamentally corrupt in both its conception and execution. *Rank Hypocrisies* is more than a *cri de coeur*. It is the best documented diagnosis of a regime that has distorted the idea of peer review beyond recognition. Only someone with the clear normative focus of a former insider could have written this work. Thucydides would be proud.
Steve Fuller, University of Warwick

The REF is right out of Havel's and Kundera's Eastern Europe: a state-administered exercise to rank academic research like hotel chains – 2 star, 3 star – dependent on the active collaboration of the UK professoriate. In crystalline text steeped in cold rage, Sayer takes aim at the REF's central claim, that it is a legitimate process of expert peer review. He provides a short history of the RAE/REF. He critiques university and national-level REF processes against actual practices of scholarly review as found in academic journals, university presses, and North American tenure procedures. His analysis is damning. If the REF fails as scholarly review, how can academics and universities continue to participate? And how can government use its rankings as a basis for public policy?

Tarak Barkawi, London School of Economics

Rank Hypocrisies offers a compellingly convincing critique of the research auditing exercise to which university institutions have become subject. Derek Sayer lays bare the contradictions involved in the REF and provides a forensic analysis of the problems and inconsistencies inherent in the exercise as it is currently constituted. A must read for all university academic staff and the fast multiplying cadre of higher education managers and, in particular, government ministers and civil servants in the Department of Business Innovation and Skills.

Barry Smart, University of Portsmouth

CONTENTS

PREFACE

I apologize in advance for the dry and sometimes legalistic style of this book, which is typical of works written with the intention of influencing public policy. But what gave rise to it was deep anger: anger as a citizen, at seeing unforgiveable amounts of scarce public money – money that could have funded research, or teaching, or student bursaries – squandered every six years on a national research audit I came to believe served no real purpose other than to keep Britain's academic elites in power; anger as a scholar, at seeing intellectual horizons narrowed, imaginations cramped and 'risky' work marginalized in the interests of maximizing universities' REF scores; and anger as a colleague, at seeing fellow academics excluded from the REF, their reputations tarnished and their confidence eroded on the basis of their own universities' internal evaluations of publications that had already passed the far more rigorous peer reviewing procedures of international publishing houses and journals. My discontent with the REF had been simmering since I returned to the UK in 2006 after 20 years teaching in Canada, but it was this treatment of colleagues that led me to pen a series of posts criticizing the REF on my blog *coastsofbohemia* during the fall of 2013. I believed it my professional and moral duty as a senior professor to take a public stand against what Peter Scott has described as 'a monster, a Minotaur that must be appeased by bloody sacrifices'.[1]

When Chris Rojek (who had been reading my blog with 'mounting incredulity') approached me with the idea of writing a short book on the REF to inaugurate the new SAGE Swifts series I grabbed the opportunity with both hands. I am grateful to be given a platform for developing my arguments at greater length. By the time I received Chris's invitation I had begun a period of sabbatical leave at the Institute for Historical Research of the University of Texas at Austin. I owe particular thanks to Mary Neuburger, Seth Garfield and

---

[1] Peter Scott, 'Why research assessment is out of control'. *Guardian*, 4 November 2013. Similar disillusion (from a one-time supporter of the RAE/REF system) is expressed by Paul Harrison, 'The perils of REF "irradiation"'. *Times Higher Education*, 24 April 2014.

(especially) Courtney Meador for making my stay as enjoyable as it was productive. This work was born, however, in the unruly new world of social media that upsets the powers that be from Ankara to Kansas,[2] and it is in that world that I have incurred my major debts. I take my title and subtitle from two tweets, one congratulating me for successfully 'calling out the rank hypocrisy of the REF', the other thanking me for having 'the integrity, courage and logic to out the insult of the REF'. I have received plentiful support on social media from many people, most of them in academia but some not, through whose efforts my posts have been widely circulated, read and commented on. Many of them will likely not agree with all conclusions of this book, but that is not the point. The point is to provoke serious public debate on matters of legitimate public concern.

Unfortunately not everyone in British universities welcomes such free debate, and UK academics do not enjoy the protection of tenure. It says a lot about the current state of British academia that several of those who wrote to me relating experiences in their own institutions asked to remain anonymous. In the circumstances I am not going to risk getting anyone – including the two colleagues who generously read and offered many useful comments on the entire manuscript – into trouble with their employers by publicly associating them with this project. But you know who you are, and you have my profound thanks for your support.

Derek Sayer
Austin, Texas
1 May 2014

---

[2] I refer to Prime Minister Recep Tayyip Erdoğan's attempts to ban Twitter and YouTube in Turkey (see 'Turkey lifts Twitter ban after court ruling'. *Guardian*, 3 April 2014) and the highly controversial policy adopted by the Regents of the University of Kansas allowing tenured faculty to be dismissed for 'improper use' of social media, including posting materials deemed 'contrary to the best interests of the university' (Eric Voeten, 'Kansas Board of Regents restricts free speech for academics'. *Washington Post*, The Monkey Cage blog, 19 December 2013).

In memory of E. P. Thompson

INTRODUCTION

The Research Excellence Framework, or REF as it is commonly called, is the most recent in a series of national assessments of research in British universities that began in 1986. The Higher Education Funding Council for England (HEFCE) and its counterparts for Scotland, Wales and Northern Ireland organize the REF on behalf of the government. These audits, previously known as Research Assessment Exercises (RAEs), have taken place at intervals of four to seven years. The change of name was intended to signal a radical shift in the method of assessment in which metrics – statistical data – would replace grading of publications by discipline-based RAE panels, making the exercise more efficient and much cheaper. In the event the universities succeeded in persuading the government that peer review remained essential to judging research quality across the disciplines and the only major change in REF 2014 from RAE 2008 – a change that was widely seen by academics as a sop to the politicians – was the addition of 'impact' as a dimension of the evaluation. These exercises are nevertheless very costly. While official estimates price the REF at around £60m, some put the bill to the taxpayer as high as £200m.[1]

Universities submit their staff to the REF in 'Units of Assessment' corresponding to 36 discipline-based REF subpanels, which may or may not mirror the organization of departments within universities. Since 1992 universities have been allowed to choose which 'research-active' staff they include in their submissions rather than having to enter all staff whose contracts include a research element, as many have argued they should be obliged to do in order to prevent gaming and provide a truer picture of institutional research profiles. Changes to HEFCE's funding formula in 2010 increased the incentives for universities to establish more systematic selection procedures for the REF and many institutions put in place elaborate 'internal REFs' as a preliminary culling device. One hundred and fifty-five institutions submitted the research of 52,077 academic staff members for assessment in REF 2014 – a slight fall on RAE 2008, but one that may conceal much higher exclusion of eligible staff in some institutions.

---

[1] See below, p. 51.

The deadline for universities to make their REF submissions was 29 November 2013. Throughout 2014, subpanels will have read the 191,232 individual research outputs that made it through universities' internal vetting procedures and graded them on a scale of 1* to 4*. The scoring of outputs is the single most important element in the overall ranking of each unit of assessment (UOA) and therefore each university, counting for 65% of the total assessment; receives a further 20% comes from 'impact' and 15% from 'research environment'. The results will be published in December 2014, with more detail to follow in Spring 2015. They will determine the level of HEFCE support for research infrastructure (so-called QR funding) that each university will receive until the next REF, which is currently expected to take place in 2020. Perhaps more importantly, they will establish a pecking order and bragging rights among universities and departments that will affect everything from their ability to compete for external research funding to their capacity to attract and retain top-notch staff and graduate students.

The REF has few equivalents elsewhere in the world and none in North America or Europe. It has proved controversial since its inception. Few would deny that RAEs initially played their part in increasing research productivity in UK universities. Certainly I would not: I left the UK for Canada in 1986 largely because I felt research and publication was neither adequately valued nor rewarded. But many – among them Sir Peter Swinnerton-Dyer,[2] author of the first 'research selectivity exercise' back in 1986 – have argued that this improvement came at inordinate cost. As we might perhaps expect, the University and College Union believes that:

> The RAE has had a disastrous impact on the UK higher education system, leading to the closure of departments with strong research profiles and healthy student recruitment. It has been responsible for job losses, discriminatory practices, widespread demoralisation of staff, the narrowing of research opportunities through the over-concentration of funding and the undermining of the relationship between teaching and research.[3]

I concur with all these points. The main thrust of this book, however, lies in a different direction. What I challenge is the claim from which the REF derives its entire authority as a mechanism for funding allocation and on which it stakes its entire legitimacy as a process of research evaluation – *the claim that it is a process of expert peer review*. It was this claim that convinced the government

---

[2]   Discussed below, pp. 83–4.

[3]   University and College Union (UCU). 'Archive: RAE 2008'. http://www.ucu.org.uk/index.cfm?articleid=1442 (accessed 23 April 2014).

to back down on its plans to replace the RAE with metrics after RAE 2008. If the claim is false, the case for metrics needs to be reconsidered – along with other ways of funding universities' research infrastructure, which might include scrapping any such centralized national research audits altogether.

Chapter 1 discusses peer review as understood and practised in various contexts in North American universities, focusing on its use in journal and book publishing, research funding competitions and tenure and promotion proceedings. Many of the features I highlight are found in comparable British settings. Had I more space, I would have liked also to discuss British promotion procedures, which are similar to those of North America in their use of external reviewers (at least at senior levels), though they often differ – I would argue, in a revealingly British way – in requiring a prima facie case to be recognized by internal committees before reviewers are approached. But the main purpose of the chapter is to establish a set of *independent international benchmarks for what constitutes peer review* against which the procedures used in the REF can be compared. Since the REF claims to evaluate individual research outputs according to international standards, this seems to me an essential starting point for any enquiry into whether it meets its declared objectives.

Chapter 2 is devoted to the REF at national level. Section 2.1 begins with a brief history of the UK's research assessment exercises from 1986 onwards and a detailed examination of the background to REF 2014, including the arguments over metrics. It ends with a brief discussion of the implications of factoring 'impact' into research evaluation. Sections 2.2 and 2.3 contain a detailed critique of the REF evaluative procedures. Among the issues raised are the narrow disciplinary remit of REF panels and their inability to evaluate interdisciplinary research, the inconsistencies of using nationally recruited panels to make judgments of comparative international excellence, the risks of replication of entrenched academic hierarchies and networks inherent in HEFCE's procedures for appointment of panel members, the unrealistic volume of work expected of panellists, the perversity of excluding all external indicators of quality from assessments, and the incompetence of REF panels to provide sufficient diversity and depth of expertise to evaluate the outputs that fall under their remit. I demonstrate the latter in detail for the History panel, my own discipline, in section 2.3. The final section of the chapter (2.4) is devoted to the changes in HEFCE's QR funding formula since 2010 and the pressures this put on individual universities to be more selective in submitting staff to the REF.

Chapter 3 focuses on what I regard as the most disturbing aspect of REF 2014, the widespread abuses that attended staff selection for the REF in individual universities. This underbelly of the REF is difficult to document (victims are often reluctant to speak on the record and universities hide their practices behind firewalls of confidentiality). I have drawn on my experience at Lancaster University, first as a Head of Department[4] appointed to improve on History's performance in RAE 2008 and latterly as a dissident who appealed against my own inclusion in the REF with the object of forcing the university to clarify the procedures and criteria it employed in staff selection. I have also made use (with permission) of the testimony of colleagues who were excluded from the REF at Lancaster, as well as published accounts of alleged REF abuses elsewhere. The opening section of the chapter (3.1) discusses Lancaster University's staff selection processes, with particular reference to the History Department; section 3.2 is a systematic demonstration of Lancaster's failure to meet HEFCE's stated criteria of transparency, consistency, accountability and inclusivity in selecting staff for REF 2014; and section 3.3 considers the situation at other universities, including Birmingham, Leicester and Warwick.

If the REF's 'peer review' processes fall so short of international standards at both the national and the local level, I ask in the concluding chapter, why should the upper echelons of British academia have been so keen to retain it? Taking off from Sir Peter Swinnerton-Dyer's suggestion that the REF has long since ceased to be a 'tolerable process' for allocating QR funding, the opening section (4.1) suggests that irrespective of their intrinsic merits or otherwise, metrics would have been an excellent predictor of most universities' performance in RAE 2008 at far lower cost and with far less damaging side effects. The point is not to defend (or advocate) metrics per se so much but to suggest that if this is the case, universities must have some considerable stake in *the REF process itself*. I conclude that the British academic establishment's tenacity in defending the REF, despite its palpable inadequacies as a process of peer review of research quality, is explained by self-interest. The REF may be dubious in the extreme as a means of evaluating the quality of individuals' research and publications, but it works admirably as a disciplinary tool for university management (4.2). It also (4.3) provides an excellent vehicle for the legitimation and replication of the country's established academic elites.

---

[4]   I should stress here that nothing said in this book rests on knowledge entrusted to me in confidence as a Head of Department.

1

BENCHMARKS

1.1 SOME ELEMENTARY PRINCIPLES OF PEER REVIEW

Few decisions are as consequential for the funding and reputation of British universities as those of REF panels. The REF casts a correspondingly long shadow over academic life in all institutions with research aspirations – above all the self-described '24 leading UK universities which are committed to maintaining the very best research' that make up the Russell Group and the '11 world class research-intensive universities' of the former 1994 Group.[1] Improving on RAE 2008 rankings was a key objective in university strategic plans in 2009–2013, and bettering REF 2014 performances is already a priority for what has (tellingly) come to be known as the next REF cycle. The imperative to maximize REF scores increasingly drives how research itself is conducted, affecting what is studied, how it is funded and where it is published. It also influences academic hiring and promotion decisions, with candidates' 'REFability' often trumping all other considerations. What began back in 1986 as a 'light touch' periodic appraisal has spawned internal university bureaucracies that *continually* monitor and increasingly seek to manage individuals' research. Once upon a time it was not thought necessary for every university department in the country to have its very own research director, but that time has long passed. So integral has the REF become to the life of UK universities that many British academics would likely have trouble imagining a world without it.

---

[1] See the groups' websites at http://www.russellgroup.ac.uk and http://www.1994group.co.uk (accessed 29 December 2013). The 1994 Group dissolved itself on 8 November 2013, following the exodus of Durham, Exeter, Queen Mary and York for the Russell Group in 2012 and the subsequent departure of Bath, Reading, St Andrews and Surrey. Warwick and LSE, now members of the Russell Group, were once members of the 1994 Group.

Strangely enough, elsewhere academic research gets evaluated and university reputations are established without such time-consuming and expensive national audits of every department's 'outputs' – as our papers, articles and books have become known in REF-speak. The British system of research appraisal reflects a very British academic culture, whose idiosyncrasy is not always appreciated by commentators at home or abroad. The RAE/REF has certainly attracted international attention, but it has seldom inspired emulation. As *Nature* once put it, '[the UK's] national research assessments have evolved over the years in ways that other agencies around the world have examined – although few, if any, have imitated the extreme extent to which the outcomes directly influence subsequent funding.'[2] While some EU states are beginning to experiment with mechanisms intended to ensure a better fit between institutional research performance and future government funding, only the former British imperial dominions of Australia, New Zealand and Hong Kong currently have anything remotely comparable in conception or scale to the REF. But the lack of a national research audit does not necessarily indicate that university research is not valued – or evaluated.

The United States – whose universities occupy seven of the top ten slots in the *Times Higher Education* World University Rankings (and 17 of the top 20 slots in the Shanghai Academic Rankings of World Universities)[3] – have no equivalent of the REF. But academics' research there is routinely evaluated, as anybody familiar with the tenure and promotion processes at any halfway decent American school will know. The crucial difference with the UK is that the mechanisms of evaluation are *internal* to the normal functioning of the academic profession rather than being externally administered by the state. Funders, whether public or otherwise, rely upon and respond to measures of reputation of both institutions and individuals that are established within the academy itself. The most important of these are bound up with peer-reviewed publication in top-drawer journals or (in the case of monographs) with leading university presses. Venue of publication operates as an initial indicator of quality, and after an article or book has been published, citations and reviews provide further indicators of impact on an academic field. The upshot is a virtuous (or, depending on your point of view, vicious) circle in which schools such as CalTech, MIT, Princeton or Harvard can attract the best researchers as indicated by their publication records, whose presence will in turn bring further prestige and research income to those same institutions. The logic

---

2   'The Greater Good'. *Nature* (editorial), 30 December 2013.

3   Times Higher Education. 'World University Rankings 2013-14', http://www.timeshighereducation.co.uk/world-university-rankings/2013-14/world-ranking; 'Academic Ranking of World Universities 2013', http://www.shanghairanking.com/ARWU2013.html (both accessed 5 January 2014). Compare 'QS World University Rankings', http://www.topuniversities.com/qs-world-university-rankings.

is explained succinctly in *The Top American Research Universities*, a publication of the State University of Arizona's Center for Measuring University Performance:

> At the point of hiring, the university first expresses its standards relative to research productivity by employing only those who show significant promise and past productivity in research. The promotion and especially the tenure process at American research universities also establish the standards for performance by keeping those who can perform at a competitive level and discouraging or dismissing those who cannot ... The best research universities make the best bets on future performance and they invest to make sure their bet is a winner.[4]

Perhaps the best place to begin this discussion is therefore with tenure, something that was abolished in Britain under the Thatcher government's 1988 Education Reform Act. Tenure in North America is 'an arrangement whereby faculty members, after successful completion of a period of probationary service, can be dismissed only for adequate cause or other possible circumstances and only after a hearing before a faculty committee'.[5] 'Other possible circumstances' would typically include severe financial exigency – tenure is meant to safeguard academic freedom, not protect against economic realities. Assuming an assistant professor has survived whatever annual or mid-probation hurdles a university puts in place, he or she would normally expect to come up for tenure after five or six years. While the record of teaching and service are important factors in tenure decisions, it is research that is critical. The most important indicator of research performance is publication. Expectations of outputs will vary according to the university. The History Department at the University of Oregon – which I have chosen as an example here because it is a good public university, but far from being an Ivy League school – is not unusual in requiring 'a published book or a completed manuscript that has been accepted for publication at a reputable press'. In appropriate areas of the discipline, articles may be submitted instead, but 'it is unlikely that fewer than six to eight would be viewed as a scholarly equivalent to a book' – a book, here, meaning a scholarly monograph based on original research. Candidates are also warned: 'Generally, books and articles should appear in highly regarded and peer-reviewed outlets'.[6]

---

4 Lombardi JV (2010) In pursuit of Number ONE. In: Capaldi ED, Lombardi JV, Abbey CW and Craig DD (eds) *The Top American Universities: 2010 Annual Report*. Tempe: Arizona State University, Center for Measuring University Performance, 7.

5 American Association of University Professors, 'Tenure', http://www.aaup.org/issues/tenure (accessed 20 December 2013).

6 University of Oregon, 'Promotion and Tenure Policies: History Department', http://academicaffairs.uoregon.edu/sites/default/files/HISTORY%20Promotion%20and%20Tenure%20Guidelines%202011.pdf (accessed 5 January 2014).

Acceptable forms of academic publication vary across disciplines in ways that are not always well understood, even within universities. In the sciences the norm – indeed, in most instances, the only form of publication that will be considered in tenure or promotion proceedings – is the scientific paper, which will often be co-authored by several members of a research team. Books count for little since they only summarize existing knowledge for teaching or popularization purposes rather than adding to it. In the humanities, on the other hand, the book is widely seen as *the* form in which the findings of a substantial research project are most fully and adequately presented, and the research monograph remains the gold standard against which other types of scholarly publication (the article, the book chapter, the edited collection, the translation, the scholarly edition, etc.) are compared. The social sciences fall somewhere in between, with economics or psychology following the science model, while cultural anthropology or the more qualitative areas of sociology are closer to the humanities. The Oregon History Department's equation of six to eight articles to one book would make no sense in chemistry or engineering, but it accurately reflects the respective values put on these forms of scholarly output in humanities disciplines. The one-size-fits-all approach of the REF for the most part ignores such differences, allowing a book to count at best as equivalent to only two articles, whatever the norms of the discipline.

Publications in the humanities are seldom multi-authored and are often much longer than those in the sciences, meaning that historians generally have fewer publications on their CV than chemists. A history article can often run to 10,000 words or more. Book chapters are also a respectable form of publication in the humanities, where the edited collections in which they are published are seen as advancing a field. Scientific papers are usually published quickly and their shelf life – the period during which they are actively being read and cited – tends to be short. The expectation in the sciences is that knowledge advances rapidly and cumulatively, so that research findings will in most cases soon be superseded by new research. In the humanities and parts of the social sciences the situation is quite different: there is usually a much longer gap between acceptance and publication, but books and articles may still be read and cited years later – indeed longevity of influence is the hallmark of a classic in its field. Walter Benjamin's *Arcades Project* (left unfinished at his death in 1940, published in 1982), Michel Foucault's *The Order of Things* (1966) or Benedict Anderson's *Imagined Communities* (1983) remain important reference points across humanities and social science disciplines. The fact that sociologists still draw on Marx, Weber and Durkheim – or philosophers on Plato and

Aristotle – does not indicate lack of progress in these disciplines so much as a different model of knowledge.

North American universities differ in the extent to which they quantify publication requirements for tenure. Many top schools do not, preferring to give flexibility to tenure committees. The Faculty of Arts and Science at New York University, for instance, takes the view that 'It is neither desirable nor possible to define an abstract and universal standard of measurement, and context may well become a criterion in judging the strength of a particular candidate'. This is very far from a licence for laxity. 'Is the candidate for tenure among the strongest in his or her field, in comparison with individuals at similar points in their careers at NYU, nationally, and, if relevant, abroad?' the guidelines ask. 'Each case must be examined in some detail by making explicit comparisons, by delineating special strengths and acknowledging limits or weaknesses. These factors must be carefully and openly weighed'.[7] Though precise expectations will vary across disciplines and between schools, it is safe to say that a candidate for tenure at any good North American university will have to meet exacting standards not only in quantity but also in quality of published research.

Crucially, whatever the university, whatever the field and whatever the form of publication, a publication invariably must have been through a *recognized process of peer review* prior to acceptance; otherwise – if it has been published on a personal website, for instance, or by a so-called 'vanity press' – it will not be eligible for consideration in tenure proceedings. The reputation of the journals and publishing houses in which articles and books appear also has a considerable bearing on how favourably publications are likely to be looked on by a tenure committee. Again, the degree to which this is formalized in terms of journal impact factors, rejection rates or rankings will vary according to the discipline and university, and open access and new forms of web-based publication have undoubtedly complicated the publishing landscape. But even where no formal ranking exists, some journals will invariably be viewed as being more prestigious than others. The same holds for monographs, with the major university presses at the top, smaller university presses next and commercial publishers bringing up the rear. Some North American schools will only accept books for tenure if published by a university press.

The link between peer review and reputation is close. Few people would argue that every article accepted by a so-called top-drawer journal or every book published by Harvard, Princeton or Chicago University Press is of a uniformly

---

[7] 'New York University Promotion and Tenure Guidelines', http://www.nyu.edu/about/policies-guidelines-compliance/policies-and-guidelines/promotion-and-tenure-guidelines.html (accessed 28 December 2013).

high standard, or would deny that excellent work gets published elsewhere. Inferior scholarship can slip through the most scrupulous of peer reviews and the outstanding can easily be missed – especially, perhaps, when it is genuinely innovative and as likely to perplex as to impress reviewers. It is nevertheless widely accepted within the North American academy that venue of publication can generally act as a proxy for quality because of the rigour of the peer review processes of the top journals and publishers and their correspondingly high rejection rates. Leading journals and presses typically commission at least three reviews for each manuscript to ensure a spread of opinion as well as to counteract possible intellectual biases. Additional reviews may be sought when a first round of assessments conflict. In the case of major university presses, the final decision on acceptance of a completed manuscript – even where there was an advance contract – is taken by an editorial board made up of experienced academics on the basis of several external reviews and the author's response. Whether for books, articles or scientific papers, the key criterion in choosing reviewers is whether or not they are *qualified by their own records of publication in the relevant field of research* to evaluate the manuscripts they are asked to read. Editors seek informed assessments by scholars who know the field well enough to evaluate the contribution in relation to its existing literatures and current debates.

Potential reviewers will be asked to declare any conflicts of interest that might cloud their judgement; immediate colleagues, research collaborators and former students (or supervisors) are usually disqualified. For major journals the process of review is ideally double-blind – the reviewer does not know the author's identity and vice versa. Nor do reviewers know each other's identities. In journals in smaller, more specialized academic fields, double-blind review can often be impractical but reviewers remain anonymous to the author and one another. With books the author's identity is usually known to reviewers but not vice versa. Because of the high degree of specialty of much academic research and the corresponding scarcity of people genuinely qualified to evaluate it, editors may consult in advance with authors over suitable reviewers – including asking if there are any people in the field who should *not* be approached because of intellectual disagreements – but the final choice of reviewers will remain unknown to the author. Reviewers provide detailed comments on manuscripts, often according to a template of headings drawn up by the journal or press. These will be conveyed to authors along with the decision to accept, reject or encourage revision and resubmission. Protecting the anonymity of reviewers is important because it allows them to express their opinions, however critical, without reservation. At the same time full communication of reviewers' comments to authors makes the reasons for publication decisions transparent and may sometimes allow those decisions to be challenged.

The same general principles of peer review apply in competitions for research grants and fellowships, which have become an important element in university reputation and income on both sides of the Atlantic. These are funded by federal agencies such as the National Endowment for the Humanities (NEH) and National Science Foundation (NSF) in the United States or Canada's Social Sciences and Humanities Research Council (SSHRC) and Natural Sciences and Engineering Research Council (NSERC), as well as by private bodies such as the Andrew W. Mellon or Wenner-Gren foundations. Major granting agencies in the UK include the seven government-funded research councils grouped under the umbrella of Research Councils UK (RCUK), whose mandate is 'investing public money in research in the UK to advance knowledge and generate new ideas which lead to a productive economy, healthy society and contribute to a sustainable world'.[8] Learned societies such as The Royal Society (for the sciences) and the British Academy (for the humanities) and charitable foundations such as the Nuffield, Wellcome and Leverhulme trusts also fund research. Although the details of their adjudication procedures will vary, all such agencies base their decisions on the advice of *a range of independent and appropriately qualified external assessors*.

The National Endowment for the Humanities, to take a prominent example, has a four-stage review process. First, applications are considered by 'a panel of outside experts in the relevant areas', whose evaluation 'informs all subsequent levels'. There are three to six evaluators per panel, chosen for 'their expertise in the relevant disciplines, topics, and areas, as well as their overall breadth of knowledge in the humanities', and each panel appraises 15–40 applications. To guard against intellectual gatekeeping, 'no evaluator may serve in consecutive years for the same grant program or on more than two convening panels in any calendar year'. More than 200 panels, involving nearly 1000 outside experts, evaluate around 5700 applications for 40 grant programs annually. Second, 'NEH's staff synthesizes the results of the outside review and prepares a slate of recommendations for the National Council on the Humanities; third, the National Council' – 'an advisory body of twenty-six members who have distinguished themselves in the humanities … nominated by the President and confirmed by the US Senate' –meets in Washington, DC, to advise the Endowment's chairman on applications and matters of policy; and fourth, the chairman considers the advice he or she has received and makes the final funding decisions.

Without compromising the confidentiality of 'applicants, evaluators, staff, and Council members', NEH goes to considerable lengths to ensure transparency and accountability in its disbursement of what are after all large sums of public money:

---

8   'About the Research Councils', http://www.rcuk.ac.uk/about/Pages/home.aspx
     (accessed 5 January 2014).

It is a matter of public information that an evaluator served on an NEH panel: The agency announces its review panels in the *Federal Register* and *lists panelists' names in its annual reports* ... NEH announces the names of award winners in each competition on its website. Importantly, *all applicants can receive upon request the evaluators' ratings and written comments*, though NEH does not provide the names of the evaluators with their comments.[9]

Peer review is not a perfect system of appraisal, and few would claim that it is. Its major drawback is that the people best qualified to be reviewers by virtue of their standing in a field are also likely to be the people with the most turf to protect and the largest axes to grind. Peer review can turn reviewers into gatekeepers unless steps are taken to avoid it. At its worst this can lead to the monopolization of whole fields by entrenched orthodoxies, marginalizing critical perspectives and ossifying disciplines. Even where this danger is avoided, peer review can discourage intellectual risk-taking on the part of authors and editors, the former because they are desperate to publish, the latter because they do not wish to offend referees. It is a truism that the highest ranked journals in a discipline are not always the places where the most challenging research is to be found. They tend to be bastions of what Thomas Kuhn called 'normal science', resistant to the scientific revolutions that periodically shift intellectual paradigms.[10] This can create serious problems for junior faculty who are doing genuinely innovative work (and discourage them from doing so), because the journals most likely to publish them are not the journals most likely to impress tenure committees.

As a long-time editor of a peer-reviewed journal[11] – as well as a scholar whose work (like everybody else's) has been hopelessly misunderstood on numerous occasions by reviewers for both journals and research councils – my response to these arguments is similar to Winston Churchill's description of democracy: 'the worst form of Government except all those other forms that have been tried from time to time'.[12] Peer review has undeniable imperfections and any sensible editor or program officer for a funding agency will be alert to them. But it remains the best procedure the academy has yet devised for

---

[9] 'NEH Grants. NEH's Application Review Process', http://www.neh.gov/grants/application-process#panel (accessed 5 January 2014). Emphasis added.

[10] Thomas S. Kuhn, *The Structure of Scientific Revolutions*. Chicago: Chicago University Press, 1962.

[11] *The Journal of Historical Sociology*, which I co-founded with Philip Corrigan in 1988. The current responsible editor is Yoke-Sum Wong.

[12] Winston Churchill, House of Commons speech, 11 November 1947, http://hansard.millbanksystems.com/commons/1947/nov/11/parliament-bill (accessed 24 February 2014).

reconciling a measure of quality control with fairness to authors and openness to new ideas. It may sometimes – perhaps often – fail in one or other of these objectives, but it is better than funding and publishing on the basis of in-house judgements alone. The latter provide no better guarantee of quality and are an obvious route for patronage and intellectual cloning. But we need to be clear on what peer review can and cannot achieve. It may, and hopefully usually does, provide a filter for weeding out work that does not meet the minimum professional standards of a scholarly community. But peer review does not provide objectivity, and still less does it guarantee truth.

Indeed, the tacit admission underlying all peer review is that *there can be no single, definitive, objective assessment of the quality of new research*. It is obviously preferable to have specialists evaluate work than people with no expertise in the field. Experts can judge a manuscript or research proposal in relation to existing knowledge and make an informed guess as to the significance of whatever it offers that is new. But the latter judgement is *always* going to be subjective – and the more genuinely novel the ideas in question are the more fallible a reviewer's judgement of their significance is likely to be, especially if that reviewer has an investment in the ideas that currently define the field, which most experts by definition will. That is the reason why leading academic journals, university presses and funding organizations always seek a *range* of expert assessments. This maximizes the possibility of faults being picked up before money is committed to a research project or a manuscript accepted for publication. But no less importantly, it also ensures that truly original research – the kind of research that changes the landscape rather than merely adding to a field – has a fighting chance of seeing the light of day.

1.2 EVALUATING RESEARCH: TENURE AND PROMOTION IN NORTH AMERICA

To have published enough peer-reviewed books, articles or papers in the right places does not guarantee tenure in North American universities even when the rest of the record (teaching and service) is satisfactory. Tenure is granted only after a more detailed appraisal, during which a candidate's publications – along with all other aspects of his or her performance since being appointed – are subjected to further evaluation. The *Promotion and Tenure Guidelines* in the History Department of the University of Oregon, to return to my earlier example, require that 'publications must make significant contributions to scholarship *in the judgment of outside referees in the candidate's field*'.[13] Published research

---

[13] University of Oregon, 'Promotion and Tenure Policies: History Department'. Emphasis added.

now goes through what is in effect a second round of peer review, designed to establish whether it was not just a contribution to scholarship (which we can assume it was by virtue of its being published in a peer-reviewed venue) but a *significant* one. This is not dissimilar to REF panels' attempt to distinguish between 2* outputs ('Quality that is recognised internationally in terms of originality, significance and rigour') and 3* ('Quality that is internationally excellent in terms of originality, significance and rigour'); so it is worth attending carefully to the procedures involved.

Since referees play so important a role in the North American tenure process and that process is so consequential for both the individual (a negative decision can be career-ending) and the university (tenured faculty may be colleagues for life), universities do not take their selection lightly. At the University of Oregon the Department Head is charged with preparing 'a list of external referees who will be invited to evaluate the research record of the candidate'. Heads are required to 'consult with members of the department and, when appropriate, members of any research institute/center with which the faculty member is affiliated' over the choice of appropriate reviewers. Candidates are then asked to prepare a separate list of referees of their own choosing. 'These processes', the guidelines stress, 'must be independent'. External reviewers 'should generally be from comparable or more highly regarded institutions. Ideally, they should be Full Professors who have *the appropriate expertise to evaluate the candidate's record'*. Conflict of interest provisions apply – a candidate cannot, for example, nominate a former PhD supervisor. A minimum of five external reviewers is required, a majority of whom must be taken from the department's list. The guidelines do not specify exactly which materials should be sent to reviewers but it is normal for all of a candidate's publications to be made available along with a CV and a statement summarizing 'scholarly accomplishments, agenda, and future plans'.[14]

The external reviewers' reports (a minimum of five, together with biographies of the reviewers)[15] are then added to materials provided by the candidate to form a tenure dossier, whose first port of call is a departmental committee that will scrutinize the file and recommend whether or not tenure is merited. The committee's report must include 'a summary and evaluation of

---

[14] University of Oregon, 'Promotion and Tenure Policies: History Department'. Emphasis added.

[15] A tenure dossier 'must include ... at least five letters from external reviewers' and 'biographies of external reviewers and a description of any known relationship between the candidate and the reviewers'. University of Oregon, 'Promotion and Tenure Policies: History Department'.

the external and internal referees' assessment of the candidate's work'. This report is made available to all tenured faculty members in advance of a department meeting, which discusses the case before proceeding to a vote by secret ballot. The Department Head then writes a statement including

> a description of the process, including any unique characteristics of the profession (e.g., books versus articles; extent of co-authorship; significance of order of names on publications, etc.). The statement also offers an opinion regarding the case for promotion and tenure that may or may not agree with the department vote.

The file – which by this point comprises the tenure dossier (including referees' reports), the departmental committee's report, the record of the department vote and the Head's statement – is then forwarded to a Dean's Advisory Committee made up of two faculty members from each of the three divisions of the university's College of Arts and Sciences (Sciences, Social Sciences and Humanities). This committee discusses and votes on the case and forwards the file to the Dean, who 'writes a letter evaluating the research, teaching, and service record of the candidate based on the contents of the file'. After writing this letter the Dean meets with the candidate and 'indicates whether or not he or she is supporting promotion ... and answers any questions with regard to the position taken on promotion and tenure'.[16] The Dean's recommendation then goes to a ten-person elected Faculty Personnel Committee, which in turn examines the file, votes on whether tenure should be granted and passes on its recommendation to the Provost. Members of the Dean's Advisory Committee and the Faculty Personnel Committee cannot participate in discussion or vote on cases from their own departments. Decisions must be *seen to be* independent. If this all seems a laborious procedure, we should perhaps recall that it is about choices between jobs for life and wrecked careers.

The final decision lies with the Provost, who has the option of meeting with candidates in difficult cases. His or her verdict can be reviewed 'only if the decision was flawed by improper procedure, by illegal discrimination, or by arbitrariness or capriciousness ... process, not standards, is the only ground for appeal'. There are once again parallels here with the REF: many UK universities similarly limited the grounds on which staff could appeal against their exclusion from REF submissions. The kinds of impropriety that might be grounds for appeal at Oregon include: 'If you feel the departmental report and outside letters have been inadequately summarized for you, or that your case has been misrepresented, or that internal bias exists and you have been treated unfairly'.

---

[16] University of Oregon, 'Promotion and Tenure Policies: History Department'.

Appellants are advised 'to get a "reality check" from a disinterested but knowledgeable third party' before embarking on any 'injudicious' action, but advice is nonetheless given on where further remedy may be sought, including the university's grievance procedure, the Oregon Bureau of Labor, the Civil Rights Division and the Oregon Courts.

Mindful, no doubt, of the risks of litigation, the university does its utmost to ensure that it is not vulnerable to challenge on procedural grounds. Care is taken to provide transparency through publication of the kind of detailed descriptions of procedures that I have been quoting (which are all posted on university websites). These guidelines are written in clear English rather than legal or bureaucratic gobbledygook and make clear to candidates exactly what should happen when. The university also ensures accountability by identifying all parties involved at every stage in the process, specifying their responsibilities with regard to the progress of the file and requiring them to produce written reports justifying their conclusions. The *only* people involved whose names will be kept from the candidate are the external referees. Should a candidate, after meeting with the Dean, believe

> aspects of your work have been misrepresented, misunderstood, or omitted, you may respond in a written statement which will accompany the materials at subsequent review levels ... This step in the review process is intended to ensure that all candidates are informed of the contents of their dossier so that they may know if their case is adequately represented from their vantage point.[17]

Details of procedure will, of course, vary between institutions. But the principles of how research is evaluated in the tenure process are pretty standard throughout North American universities. Only peer-reviewed publications are eligible for consideration, and whether or not formal journal or publisher rankings are employed, the venue of publication matters. Peer review is understood in the sense set out in the first part of this chapter. In the course of tenure proceedings, publications are further appraised by several external reviewers specifically appointed for the purpose, who are chosen not only for their eminence in the profession – they are usually expected to be of Full Professor rank – but above all for their *specialist knowledge of the candidate's field* as reflected in their own publication record. Care is taken to ensure that reviewers are 'arm's length', but candidates are usually given some say in their choice. There is always a range of external appraisals – research evaluation for tenure

---

[17] University of Oregon, Office of Academic Affairs, 'Evaluation and Promotion – Tenure Track'. http://academicaffairs.uoregon.edu/evaluation-and-promotion-tenure-track (accessed 21 April 2014).

(or promotion) purposes will never be left in the hands of a single individual, no matter how expert or eminent that person may be. While reviewers' identity will be kept anonymous, candidates are provided with at least a summary of their comments (to which they will have the opportunity to respond).

Departmental colleagues often have input into the tenure process, which may, as in Oregon, be expressed through a formal vote. At the University of Alberta, where I sat on the Arts Faculty Evaluation Committee (which considered all promotion and tenure cases) for seven years, Heads of Department were required to take soundings of the opinion of tenured colleagues, but no departmental vote was taken – perhaps to avoid the politicking that is widely seen as marring American tenure processes. In cases where there was a difference between the departmental view and the recommendations of external assessors, the committee was usually more inclined to go with the externals. Institutional cultures differ. The ultimate decision, however, is invariably made at a level higher than the department, on the basis of recommendations by faculty and university committees that have *independently* scrutinized the cumulative file. Such committees are usually cross-disciplinary in composition, often have some elected members and exclude members from discussing and voting on cases from their own departments. The process is governed by clear and explicit rules, which are designed to ensure that evaluations are both competent and fair. In most cases this framework will have been drawn up through collective bargaining with staff associations or unions and enshrined in a legally binding faculty agreement that can only be modified through formal renegotiation.

In most North American universities tenure automatically entails promotion to Associate Professor; so there is no separate procedure involved.[18] The publication expectations for promotion to Full Professor are obviously higher – the Oregon History Department, for instance, requires a second book (or equivalent), together with other evidence of

> professional standing and impact on the scholarly field, as demonstrated by the evaluations of external reviewers, awards, membership on boards of journals and professional organizations, and the like; external grant funding; conference attendance and presentations; and other activities that are signs of professional regard, including editorial activities and providing promotion reviews for other institutions.[19]

---

[18] Harvard University is a prominent exception, only offering tenured appointments at the Full Professor level.

[19] University of Oregon. 'Promotion and Tenure Policies: History Department'.

External reviewers of publications for Full Professor promotions are expected to provide highly detailed reports. When I recently participated in such a review for Harvard University I was not only asked to comment in detail on the two books and six articles sent to me, but also to rank the candidate relative to five other named scholars in the field, giving my 'frank advice and candid opinion' of their respective merits.[20] Expectations of the impact of publications on a field will also be significantly higher than the expectations for promotion to Associate Professor, and committees may want to see evidence of citations of papers and reviews of books. But the procedures through which published work is evaluated and the committee structures involved are similar to those employed for tenure and need not detain us further here.

Let me be clear from the start: I am *not* against the evaluation of research. Nor do I oppose universities' right as employers to act upon such evaluations to advance or hold back individuals' career progression within the institution – up to and including dismissal for breach of contract, if necessary, so long as this is done through due process of the sort enshrined in most North American faculty agreements. All I insist upon is that such evaluations should be made on *proper academic grounds* and through the use of *proper academic procedures*, including, above all, *proper peer review*. Defenders of the UK's national research assessment system like to describe it as a process of 'international benchmarking'. What I have set out in this chapter are some international benchmarks against which to measure the evaluative procedures employed by HEFCE and individual British universities in the context of REF 2014. The central claim of the UK's research evaluation system has always been that it 'is essentially a peer review process'.[21] Judged against the standards outlined in this chapter, I shall argue, that statement is indefensible.

---

[20] Private communication from a Department Chair at Harvard University.

[21] HEFCE, *Review of research assessment: Report by Sir Gareth Roberts to the UK funding bodies* (May 2003), 4, http://www.ra-review.ac.uk/reports/roberts/roberts_summary. pdf (accessed 19 March 2014).

2

POTEMKIN'S VILLAGE

2.1 THE GREAT METRICS DEBATE: FROM RAE TO REF

The UK's first 'research selectivity exercise', mounted in 1986 by the University Grants Committee (UGC) – the body that had been the interface between universities and the state since 1919 – was a modest affair. The UGC's 37 subject sub-committees assessed each department on the basis of a 'four-page general description of its strengths' and five research outputs on which it was 'content for its total output to be assessed'. They also drew freely on knowledge gathered through periodic departmental visitations. Judged by today's standards this looks a laughably amateurish process, but its architect Sir Peter Swinnerton-Dyer told *Times Higher Education* in 2013 that 'no one has ever seriously doubted that it was "adequate for getting the estimates roughly right"'. 'This is not surprising', he went on, since 'if the best five elements are good, the overall quality is probably good as well'. Swinnerton-Dyer opposed gathering information about departments' total publications or evaluating individual researchers, the former on the grounds that it would 'only encourage the production of low-quality papers' and the latter because it would require 'an absolutely intolerable level of work'. In his view, all later versions of the RAE, including REF 2014, 'try to produce more information in more detail than a tolerable process could do'.[1]

The same 1988 Education Reform Act that stripped British academics of tenure abolished the UGC along with its subject committees. In the 1989 research selectivity exercise their place was taken by nearly 70 specially convened review panels, which evaluated 152 subject-based UOAs – significantly upping the scale and costs of the enterprise. Under pressure from the Committee of Vice-Chancellors and Principals, who believed the 1986 formula did not allow departments to showcase their strengths, Swinnerton-Dyer allowed universities

---

[1] Quoted in Paul Jump, 'Evolution of the REF'. *Times Higher Education*, 17 October 2013.

to submit two outputs for each staff member rather than the previous five outputs per department (though he thought it 'a silly idea').[2] This principle became a backbone of all subsequent RAE/REF exercises, with the number of outputs required per staff member rising to four in 1996. A scale for scoring outputs based on 'necessarily "woolly" universal definitions for each point related to national and international standards'[3] became another staple of the process. The 1989 RAE also collected data on the volume of each department's publications (a requirement that was dropped in 1996), research grant income and research student numbers. Though the details would be (constantly) refined through successive assessment exercises, many of the defining features of the RAE/REF regime were already in place by 1989.

But the game changed dramatically with the abolition of the distinction between universities and polytechnics in 1992. Until then the UGC and its successor the UFC (University Funding Committee, replaced by HEFCE in 1992) only disbursed around 40% of their research budget through research selectivity exercises. The rest was allocated on the basis of research grant income, volume of external research contracts and staff and student numbers – a commonsensical distribution that reconciled support for all universities as research institutions with a measure of concentration in areas of proven excellence. But with the end of the binary system any continued funding of research according to staff or student numbers would have diverted resources from research-oriented universities to teaching-focused former polytechnics. Under its new Director of Policy, Bahram Bekhradnia, HEFCE took two crucial steps to avoid this. First, it ended all research support based on staff or student numbers and instead allocated its research budget according to the outcomes of Research Assessment Exercises (as the research selectivity exercises were renamed). For this reason this budget became known as Quality-related or QR funding. Second, it permitted universities to submit only staff deemed 'research-active' to the RAE. While both measures made excellent sense at the time, they would be the source of major problems in the future. Distributing all HEFCE research funding as QR turned the RAE into a high-stakes game between universities, within which staff selection would become an increasingly important strategic element.

With the increase in the scale and stakes of the exercise the old amateurish ethos had to go. In Bekhradnia's words, the RAE needed to become 'much more robust and rigorous ... when so much was at stake, we were going to be subject

---

[2] Swinnerton-Dyer, quoted in Jump, 'Evolution of the REF'. Swinnerton-Dyer was by this time Chief Executive of the Universities Funding Council (UFC), the successor to the UGC.

[3] Jump, 'Evolution of the REF'. The word 'woolly' is Swinnerton-Dyer's.

to legal challenge if we didn't do it right'.[4] The RAE 1992 results were indeed challenged in court and the judge 'warned that administrative law was moving very fast in the direction of transparency and it was no good experts simply saying they used their expert judgement to decide whether this was a good or bad submission'.[5] Thereafter HEFCE was careful to be (somewhat) more open about its processes and – rather less successfully – urged the same of universities. Inevitably this led to greater bureaucracy. In 1992, 63 subpanels evaluated around 2800 submissions in 72 UOAs; by 2008, 67 subpanels were being supervised by 15 main panels. From 1996 subpanels published their assessment criteria and working methods in advance. Bekhradnia believes that the resulting proliferation of rules proved a mixed blessing, encouraging gaming as much as it did fairness. In his view,

> The ideal RAE would be one where people wake up and find they got a score but don't know how they got it. If being explicit helps people to change their practices in a way that makes things better then that is desirable, but I doubt if that is the case.[6]

One of the concerns of the Roberts review that followed RAE 2001 was 'an increased risk that as HEIs' [Higher Education Institutions'] understanding of the system becomes more sophisticated, games-playing will undermine the exercise'.[7]

Others were more worried about the spiralling costs of the enterprise. A 2009 report calculated the costs of RAE 2008 to higher education institutions at just over £47m – a nominal average of £612,828 per institution and £1127 per staff member – across English universities alone. Factored into these figures were 'a variety of activities which require significant time and resource in terms of staff involvement, systems, co-ordination and internal governance', including

> the validation of publications information, the creation of tailored abstracts and participation in departmental and faculty review groups. Furthermore, many institutions engage in activities which go "above and beyond" the minimum requirements of the RAE process in order to improve the quality of their submission, including strategic recruitment and external peer review.[8]

---

4 Bahram Bekhradnia, quoted in Jump, 'Evolution of the REF'.

5 Jump, 'Evolution of the REF'.

6 Quoted in Jump, 'Evolution of the REF'.

7 HEFCE. *Review of research assessment. Report by Sir Gareth Roberts to the UK funding bodies* (May 2003), 4.

8 PA Consulting Group, *RAE 2008 Accountability Review* (HEFCE, May 2009), 18–19, http://www.hefce.ac.uk/pubs/rereports/year/2009/rae2008accountabilityreview/ (accessed 3 February 2014).

We can add a further £12m in HEFCE's costs of administering the show, giving a total bill for the 2008 RAE at £60m.[9] Many academics would argue that the opportunity costs are even more significant: *this is all staff time that could have been devoted to actually doing research instead of monitoring it.* Two years earlier, and quite independently of HEFCE (to whom, according to Bekhradnia, it came 'completely out of the blue'),[10] HM Treasury had also come to the conclusion that this was all getting to be too much. In his 2006 Budget Chancellor of the Exchequer Gordon Brown announced that the government intended to move to a 'metrics-based system for assessing research quality' after RAE 2008.[11] A working group chaired by David Eastwood, HEFCE chief executive designate, and Sir Alan Wilson, Director-General for Higher Education at the Department for Education and Skills, was set up to consult on the government's proposal.

HEFCE published the results of this consultation in January 2007. There were 287 responses, of which 113 came from UK higher education institutions and 74 from subject associations ranging from the British Sociological Association to the Biosciences Federation. A very broad cross-section of the British academic establishment took part in the exercise, including umbrella organizations such as the Russell Group, the 1994 Group and the Alliance of Non-aligned Universities, not to mention the British Academy and The Royal Society. To say that the government's proposed move to a metrics-based system met with little enthusiasm would be putting it mildly. There was overwhelming opposition to making any changes to evaluative procedures in RAE 2008, with 158 out of 193 respondents taking the view that 'none of the 2008 panels should alter their published criteria and working methods in order to make greater use of metrics'. A majority of respondents (including the Russell Group) also 'felt that the RAE outcomes should continue to inform funding decisions for a significant period beyond 2008'.

When it came to the future, opinion was more mixed but the general tenor of the response was decidedly sceptical. Most respondents rejected any metrics based purely on inputs (e.g. research grant income) in favour of 'the inclusion of an indicator to reflect the quality of research outputs, and a large majority of these felt that some kind of peer evaluation was the only form of assessment that could deliver this effectively'. Universities UK (UUK) 'spoke for a large majority' in arguing that 'Most of the metrics suggested to date are proxy indicators of quality, rather than measures of quality. Therefore, expert assessment must also continue within the process, for example overseeing the validity and

---

[9]   Zoe Corbyn, 'Structural adjustments'. *Times Higher Education*, 14 May 2009.

[10] Quoted in Jump, 'Evolution of the REF'.

[11] 'Budget surprise signals research funding revamp', *Times Higher Education*, 24 March 2006.

selection of the metrics, interpreting and, where necessary, moderating their outcomes.' While some respondents (among them the 1994 Group) 'acknowledged the potential for bibliometrics to provide an indicator of output quality ... there was broad agreement that existing indices would not necessarily be appropriate for these purposes, and that bibliometrics in general would be more relevant to some disciplines than to others'. Others 'entirely rejected the use of bibliometric indicators, typically arguing that these cannot be used to replace the peer review process wholly'.

Among the arguments against bibliometrics were: 'that journal impact factors and citations can be misleading as indicators of research quality; that review articles are cited frequently but often do not contain primary research; that time-lags between publication and citation can cause problems for bibliometrics; and that the present databases are inaccurate'. RCUK noted 'significant variation in the usefulness of bibliometrics even within the STEM[12] subjects', cautioning: 'the research councils have made some progress in the use of such analyses for these subjects at broad ('super UoA') levels ... but such analyses should not be used in isolation'. Respondents generally 'did not support separate assessment methods for STEM subjects and other subjects' and were 'virtually unanimous in advocating some form of peer evaluation as the main basis for assessing non-STEM subjects'. For all these and other reasons there was 'significant consensus that further work would be needed before any wholly metrics-based model could be made to work'.[13]

Faced with this rejection of its proposals by the massed ranks of the academic great and good, the government backed off – a little. Acknowledging the concerns that had been voiced, it now proposed to replace the RAE with a two-track process pending 'development of metrics fit for the purpose of assessment in areas where they are currently less well developed'. In science, technology and engineering subjects, it was decided, 'Assessment will be based on a rating derived from income, postgraduate student and bibliometric indicators, with expert advice on the weighting of these elements' by 'no more than seven expert advisory groups'. For all other subjects (including mathematics) 'Assessment will be based on a rating derived from a basket of metrics containing research income and postgraduate student metrics, together with expert review of selected research outputs, and with expert advice on the weighting of all these elements'. Despite this backtracking it was promised that 'The review

---

[12] STEM subjects: science, technology, engineering and mathematics.

[13] All quotations from Department for Education and Skills, *Dfes Consultation on the Reform of Higher Education Research Assessment and Funding: Summary of Responses*. January 2007.

of outputs will be significantly less burdensome for higher education institutions and their researchers than the current RAE process'.[14] In the buzzword of the time, peer review was to be 'light touch'. Some might see this as a contradiction in terms (Bekhradnia later observed: 'If the assessment is going to be fair and comprehensive and sophisticated ... it is unlikely to be light touch').[15] Eastwood and HEFCE were charged with delivering the nuts and bolts of this new Research Excellence Framework (REF), as it was renamed to make clear to everybody how different it was from the RAE.

What is remarkable – but not altogether surprising to anyone familiar with the tenacity of British elites and their ability to ride the winds of change – is that under guise of working out the details of its implementation this new two-track model of assessment was almost entirely abandoned over the next two years. In a second HEFCE consultation that closed in February 2008, UUK, the Russell Group, the 1994 Group, The Royal Society and the British Academy all questioned the use of dual forms of assessment for science and arts subjects, while several learned societies (significantly including The Royal Society, the Royal Academy of Engineering and the Royal Astronomical Society) reiterated the pitfalls of relying on citation data and the desirability of maintaining some form of peer review across the board. The Russell Group called for 'an extension of the existing timetable by at least 12 months' because 'The robustness of proposals is considered to be more important than the proposed timescale'.[16] In other contexts, like its own website, the Russell Group has been more than happy to recognize citations as 'the acid test of whether research is being taken seriously',[17] which raises the suspicion that more than the methodology of research evaluation was at stake in these debates. Later that month RCUK, too, demanded a single system of assessment for science and non-science subjects that included some form of 'light-touch peer review'. HEFCE's proposals, it said, were 'not acceptable in their current form'. Bekhradnia, who was by now running the Higher Education Policy Institute, helpfully let it be known that 'he could not think of a previous case where one agency of a government department had so publicly criticised the proposals of another'.[18]

14 *Dfes Consultation on the Reform of Higher Education Research Assessment.*

15 Quoted in Corbyn, '"Structural adjustments'.

16 Zoe Corbyn, 'REF consultation: academe's concerns'. *Times Higher Education*, 14 May 2008.

17 'Research at Russell Group Universities'. http://www.russellgroup.ac.uk/research/ (accessed 12 February 2014).

18 Zoe Corbyn, 'Plans for RAE metrics draw fire from research councils'. *Times Higher Education*, 28 February 2008.

Three months later the government agreed to a year's delay in imple-menting the REF.[19] It had also apparently had second thoughts on dual-track assessment. 'A new metrics-based assessment framework will make greater use of statistical indicators', it was announced, 'helping reduce the need for peer review. So *for all subjects*, the assessment will include metrics-based indicators, including bibliometric indicators of quality wherever appropriate, *as well as input from expert panels*'. Nobody was fooled by this face-saving formula. Remarking that the new plans were 'unrecognisable' from the REF concept of a year earlier, Bekhradnia gleefully commented that 'What we now seem to have ... is peer review informed by metrics ... which represents a natural evolution of the research assessment exercise'.[20] Later he would describe the government's approach to metrics as 'completely batty'.[21] David Eastwood spun it as best he could, claiming: 'A single framework with vari-able geometry, appropriately combining metrics, expert assessment and peer review, is the prize that is within our grasp'. He announced 'an ambitious programme over the next 12 months' that would involve 'a thorough and rigorous pilot exercise in generating bibliometric quality profiles to evalu-ate options' and 'robust but less burdensome forms of peer review, both to complement metrics and to give judgments where metrics are silent or insuf-ficiently well developed'.[22]

In the following months, opponents of metrics lost no opportunity to drive the knife home. Bekhradnia warned of the legal pitfalls awaiting HEFCE if it got the balance of numbers and peer review wrong:

> The critical question is, which is the primary driver? When I was at Hefce and in charge of the RAE we didn't move without getting legal advice about the likely success of any challenge over what we were doing. I would be very surprised if the lawyers didn't advise that you can't have a system based primarily on data, where the results of the metrics could be overturned by the judgements of panels.
>
> Anyone who found that their scores based on metrics had been lowered would sue, and probably win. But you can have a system based on peer review in

---

[19] Zoe Corbyn, 'Launch of REF to be delayed a year'. *Times Higher Education*, 10 April 2008.

[20] Zoe Corbyn, 'DIUS abandons plans for different REF systems to judge sciences and arts'. *Times Higher Education*, 24 April 2008. Emphasis added.

[21] John Morgan, 'Bahram Bekhradnia: a critical friend delivers home truths'. *Times Higher Education*, 11 April 2013.

[22] David Eastwood, 'We can win the double'. *Times Higher Education*, 29 May 2008.

which data is among the evidence that is taken into account. There is a really important distinction here that hasn't been clarified.[23]

In August 2008 the chairs of 11 RAE subpanels expressed 'concern about the reduced influence of peer review under the forthcoming research excellence framework (REF)' and went on to 'raise worries about the rigid application of metrics, such as citation counts, to assess quality and determine funding'.[24] Such a collective intervention was unprecedented. Their message was rammed home in the formal overviews produced by RAE 2008 panels and published in January 2009, with the computer science, sociology, language research, education, history and economics panels all expressing scepticism about bibliometrics and defending the continued need for peer review. The law panel was 'unanimous' that 'detailed peer review of outputs is the only method that will attract the confidence of our discipline'.[25] Six months later HEFCE threw in the towel. 'We just don't think bibliometrics are sufficiently mature at this stage to be used in a formulaic way or, indeed, to replace expert review', explained REF project manager Graeme Rosenberg, though he added that 'there is still scope for bibliometrics to *inform* the assessment process'.[26] That scope would turn out to be very limited indeed.

When HEFCE published its final proposals on 23 September 2009 they were greeted with the headlines 'RAE sequel looks strangely familiar'[27] and 'It's evolution, not revolution for the REF'. This was the last outcome anybody would have predicted 18 months, let alone three years previously. 'While we remain concerned to reduce the burden of the assessment', the document admitted, 'we believe we have exhausted the main options for any radically different alternative approach'. In the event there were only two major changes from RAE 2008. First, the number of panels and subpanels was much reduced (though the number of assessors HEFCE expected to use remained about the same). Bekhradnia – who expressed 'great relief' at the retreat from metrics – thought

---

[23] Quoted in John Gill, 'Peer review must be at the heart of REF, expert says'. *Times Higher Education*, 17 July 2008.

[24] Zoe Corbyn, 'Keep peer review at REF core, chairs warn'. *Times Higher Education*, 28 August 2008.

[25] John Gill, 'Keep peer input in REF, urge panels'. *Times Higher Education*, 8 January 2009.

[26] Quoted in Zoe Corbyn, 'Hefce backs off citations in favour of peer review in REF'. *Times Higher Education*, 18 June 2009. Emphasis added.

[27] Zoe Corbyn, 'RAE sequel looks strangely familiar'. *Times Higher Education*, 23 September 2009.

this move 'understandable and brave' but worried that it might be 'damaging to the credibility of the exercise if large numbers thought that they were being judged by people without the competence to do so'.[28] We shall see that his concern was well founded.

The second change was more dramatic and less expected. For the first time in any research assessment exercise the economic and social *impact* of research was now to be measured, independent of its quality. Indeed, HEFCE announced, this would count for 25% of the total assessment (the figure would later be reduced to 20%). This idea – which had formed no part of the previous consultations on what should replace the RAE – first publicly surfaced at an Academy of Social Sciences conference in London two months earlier when Graeme Rosenberg raised it as a 'starting-point' for discussion. 'We strengthen our case for public investment in research if we can show that university research has actually produced a clear, visible impact and that the system itself recognises and rewards … [it]', he urged. 'If you don't give impact a big enough weighting, you have no influence on outcomes. We have got to show the Government that impact is an important part of the REF'.[29] Though there were to be further token consultations and much minor tinkering with the details of the framework set out in September 2009, impact would prove to be the one thing that was non-negotiable.

For reasons of space I shall say little in this book about impact, except insofar as introducing it into the REF provided additional reasons, based on pure numbers, for some universities to exclude eligible individuals from UOA submissions. This should not be taken to mean that I consider the issue unimportant. On the contrary, I take it as further evidence of the British academic establishment's willingness to sell its birthright for a mess of pottage. In his discussion of US research university rankings John V. Lombardi makes the important point that 'One of the characteristics of much new knowledge is that *it has no useful application at the moment of its creation*':

> When we identify something new, some characteristic of the physical, biological, or cultural world previously unknown or imperfectly understood, the discovery may appear trivial or bizarre to some observers. The utility of research discoveries often appears much later when others have extended the discovery into related areas of research, broadening the significance, and developing a full understanding that transforms the original invention into products or processes

---

[28] Quotations from Zoe Corbyn, 'It's evolution, not revolution for REF'. *Times Higher Education*, 24 September 2009.

[29] Quoted in Zoe Corbyn, 'Impact may account for 30% of researchers' marks in REF'. *Times Higher Education*, 23 July 2009.

that change the way we live, create substantial economic or social value, or provide a major national competitive advantage.

This is why, he explains, the top American research universities require 'a continuous process of quality control and improvement to sustain long-term research productivity'.[30]

Long-term impact cannot be measured within REF timelines or be established by such fatuous indicators as how many people attend a public lecture or listen to a radio interview: things British universities now require their faculty members to document for possible REF purposes. Sir Peter Swinnerton-Dyer was distinctly unimpressed by the whole charade, dismissing impact assessment as 'a licence for lying' since the evidence is 'uncheckable'.[31] But how *should* one measure the global social and economic impact – for good or for ill – of Adam Smith's *Wealth of Nations* (first published 1776), Karl Marx's *Capital* (published 1867) or John Maynard Keynes's *General Theory of Employment, Interest and Money* (published 1936)? At what point in the 20th century might a hypothetical REF have begun to register the non-academic impact of the four papers Albert Einstein published in 1905, together with early-20th-century discoveries in theoretical physics by Rutherford, Bohr, Marie and Pierre Curie and others that were gobbledygook to almost everyone at the time? 6 August 1945, perhaps?

There can be no guarantee that *any* academic research is going to have impact; not knowing the results in advance is precisely what makes it research. But what is most worrying is that because the REF gives impact a significant enough weighting to affect the outcomes of its appraisals, it will also come to shape the kind of research that gets done. Everybody will pay lip service to the need to support pure research, just as they always genuflect to the virtues of interdisciplinarity. But when each individual 'impact case study' counts for a substantially greater portion of the overall UOA score than the research outputs of any individual faculty member, and the research underpinning the impact needs to be of only 2* quality – which in the case of an output would now attract *no* HEFCE funding – the fear is that universities will prioritize support for research that appears likely to have measurable short-term impact because this is what promises the greatest rewards for the least risk. Tails will increasingly wag dogs as departments' research agendas – and hiring practices – become driven by the lure of quick bucks made from instant impact. This is the shameful price British academia has paid the politicians in the Faustian bargain that

---

30 Lombardi, 'In Pursuit of Number ONE', 4–5.

31 Quoted in Jump, 'Evolution of the REF'.

allowed them to keep the bizarre system of panel appraisal of outputs they persist in calling peer review. It is to this system that I shall now turn.

2.2 SELECTION, COMPOSITION AND WORKLOAD OF REF PANELS

The mandate of REF 2014, HEFCE tells us, is 'assessing the quality of research in UK higher education institutions' through 'a process of expert review'. The slippage from 'peer review', the mantra of the anti-metrics campaign, to 'expert review', the term used throughout the official REF documents, was seamless. This process, we are told, will: (1) 'inform the selective allocation of research funding to HEIs on the basis of excellence'; (2) 'provide benchmarking information and reputational yardsticks' and (3) 'provide accountability for public investment in research and demonstrate its benefits'.[32] Not only is this a dauntingly – some might say, an inordinately – ambitious set of goals, it is also a logistically formidable task. In all, 155 higher education institutions made submissions to the 2014 REF, entering the research of 52,077 staff members for assessment.[33] Between 29 November 2013 (the closing date for submissions) and December 2014 (when HEFCE proposes to publish outcomes),[34] 191,232 individual papers, articles, book chapters and books will have had to be read 'by panel members and/or assessors … with a level of detail sufficient to contribute to the formation of a robust sub-profile for all the outputs in that submission'.[35] The National Endowment for the Humanities' 5700 applications for its 40 grant programs is very small beer by comparison. Yet curiously, the REF uses around the same number of assessors *in total* as NEH.[36] This fact alone should lead us to question just how 'robust' – let alone how fair – such a process of evaluation can be.

---

[32] HEFCE, *REF2014: Units of Assessment and Recruitment of Expert Panels*, paras 7, 8.

[33] HEFCE, 'REF submissions received' (5 December 2013). http://www.hefce.ac.uk/ news/newsarchive/2013/news85247.html (accessed 7 January 2014).

[34] HEFCE, 'REF2014: Timetable'. http://www.ref.ac.uk/timetable/ (accessed 7 January 2014).

[35] *REF 2014: Units of Assessment*, para 121. Figure from REF website, 'Submissions'. February 2014. http://www.ref.ac.uk/subguide/ (accessed 16 February 2014).

[36] NEH uses 'almost a thousand' external experts (see p. 11 above). I am assuming an average REF panel membership of 20 and an additional 5 academic assessors for each of the 36 REF subpanels to arrive at a figure of 900. HEFCE gave a figure of 810 members for all panels in July 2011; these did not include additional assessors. See HEFCE, *REF2014: Analysis of Panel Membership*, para 12. The precise figures don't matter here; it is the contrast of orders of magnitude that I want to highlight.

REF 2014 is 'managed by the REF team based at HEFCE and overseen by the REF Steering Group, consisting of representatives of the four funding bodies'.[37] Four Main Panels cover medicine and the life sciences (Panel A); the physical sciences, mathematics and engineering (Panel B); geography, the social sciences, business and law (Panel C); and the arts and humanities (Panel D). The actual research assessments are carried out by 'discipline-based expert [sub]panels … [which] work under the leadership and guidance of … Main Panels A, B, C and D'.[38] The Main Panels are expected to articulate 'the criteria and working methods for the group of subpanels under [their] remit', ensuring effective consultation with 'the academic community' as well as with 'stakeholders from the private, public and third sectors who are informed by, make use of or benefit from academic research in the disciplines covered by the panel'. Main Panels 'work with the subpanels … to calibrate the assessment standards between subpanels and ensure the consistent application across the framework of the overall assessment standards', 'sign off the assessment outcomes' produced by the subpanels for each institution and 'produce a final report on the state of research in the disciplines covered by the subpanels and its wider benefits'.[39] All subpanel chairs sit on the relevant Main Panel alongside 'additional members with expertise in the use, application and wider benefits of research' and 'additional members with international expertise'. The job of the latter is 'to contribute especially to the development of main panel criteria that reflect international standards, and to provide assurance during the assessment phase that subpanels adhere to internationally referenced standards'.[40]

One disciplinary subpanel covers each UOA. There are 36 UOAs in all: as we have seen, a substantial reduction on the 67 used in the 2008 RAE. The number of Main Panels was even more drastically reduced, from 15 to 4. Though the claimed intention of this change was 'primarily to enable greater consistency across the exercise, and to help reduce burden', concern was expressed in a HEFCE consultation that some subpanels 'would lack coherence or would be too diverse (particularly in the humanities)', while others might not 'include sufficient breadth and depth of expertise to produce robust assessments and carry the confidence of the community'.[41] It has also been argued that reducing the range of subpanels created particular problems for interdisciplinary work.

---

[37] See http://www.ref.ac.uk (accessed 6 January 2013).

[38] HEFCE, *REF2014: Panel Criteria and Working Methods*, para 22.

[39] *REF 2014: Units of Assessment*, para 25. The 'third sector' is the voluntary, nonprofit sector, as distinct from either public or private sectors.

[40] *REF 2014: Units of Assessment*, para 33.

[41] *REF 2014: Units of Assessment*, para 14. Don't university administrators just love the word 'robust'?

The size of subpanels ranges between 10 and 30 members depending on 'the scale and diversity of the panel's remit'. Subpanels include not only 'practicing researchers of suitable personal standing who collectively have an appropriate breadth of research expertise' (academic members), but also 'members from the private, public or third sectors with expertise in commissioning, applying or making use of research' (user members).[42] This innovation reflects REF 2014's concern with impact.[43]

Subpanels may also contain 'additional experts to assist ... in assessing submissions, to ensure the panels have sufficient breadth and depth of expertise for this task'. These are termed 'assessors' as distinct from 'members'. While most assessors are drawn from communities of research users and are expected to contribute to the evaluation of impact, panels may also recruit assessors who are 'practicing researchers with specific expertise, to contribute in particular to the assessment of outputs'. These are appointed either to cover gaps in a subpanel's expertise or to ensure that 'the workload of assessing potentially large volumes of outputs can be spread across a sufficient number of people'.[44] Such assessors replace the external 'specialist advisers' used in RAE 2008

> where a subpanel has to assess significant work in a sub-disciplinary area that either the members collectively do not feel qualified to cover ... or which crosses traditional disciplinary boundaries in such a way that they judge it would be best assessed by someone with interdisciplinary or cross-disciplinary expertise that they do not have.[45]

The upshot – contrasting sharply with the peer review procedures examined in Chapter 1 – is that *all evaluation in REF 2014 is done in-house*.[46]

HEFCE appointed Main Panel chairs on the basis of open competition. Subpanel chairs were recruited competitively, but only appointed 'after taking advice from the Main Panel chairs'. Applicants for subpanel chair positions were also required to provide 'statements of endorsement by subject associa-

---

[42] *REF 2014: Units of Assessment*, para 36.

[43] Inclusion of 'an explicit element to assess the non-academic impact of research' is singled out under the heading 'Key changes since RAE 2008' itemized in HEFCE, *REF 2014: Assessment Framework and Guidance on Submissions (updated to include addendum published in January 2012)*, para 46 (e).

[44] *REF 2014: Units of Assessment*, para 37.

[45] HEFCE, *RAE2008: Units of Assessment and Recruitment of Panel Members* (July 2004), para 32.

[46] The only exception is 'outputs submitted in languages that the subpanel is unable to assess'. *REF 2014: Assessment framework*, para 46 (j).

tions and/or other organisations that demonstrate the individual's standing in the community'.[47] This proviso would have considerably narrowed the field while giving professional associations and learned societies – for good or ill – an effective veto over who chairs the REF committees that evaluate their disciplines. Subpanel chairs in turn 'advised' on the appointment of subpanel members and subpanel members advised on the appointment of assessors, making this a very British process of sponsored recruitment within which existing disciplinary networks and hierarchies could cosily replicate themselves.[48] It comes as no surprise to find that representatives from Russell Group and 1994 Group universities overwhelmingly preponderated among the academic members of REF panels. As HEFCE nicely put it, 'Main and subpanel chairs were enlisted through an open recruitment process and panel members were appointed through a nominations process'.[49] The distinction is an important one. The process through which those who did the actual reading and scoring of outputs were recruited was *not* 'open'.

'Individual UK HEIs and groups within or subsidiaries of individual UK HEIs' were not allowed to nominate subpanel members – presumably to avoid any perception of conflict of interest – but just about everybody else was. HEFCE provided a surreal list of 1950 'academic associations and other bodies with an interest in research' and encouraged 'any other association or organisation with a clear interest in the conduct, quality, funding or wider benefits of publicly funded research' to submit nominations. Side by side with learned societies and professional associations, the list included private companies (such as Barclays, Bentley Motors and British American Tobacco), charities and voluntary organizations (Amnesty International, Help the Aged and Oxfam) and government agencies (Department for Business, Innovation and Skills, Her Majesty's Revenue and Customs and HM Treasury) – evidently nobody saw any potential conflicts of interest here.[50] This document can have been of no practical use in identifying potential panel members *academically* qualified to assess the UK's research outputs, but as an exercise in laborious but impressive pointlessness it captures the spirit of the REF perfectly. It also testifies to the poverty of politicians' understanding of the nature of academic research and – rather more disturbingly – the willingness of HEFCE and the British academic establishment

[47] *REF 2014: Units of Assessment*, paras 43, 44.

[48] *REF 2014: Units of Assessment*, paras 53, 54.

[49] 'REF 2014: Panel Membership'. http://www.ref.ac.uk/panels/panelmembership/ (accessed 8 January 2014).

[50] 'REF2014: Nominating Bodies'. http://www.ref.ac.uk/panels/panelmembership/ (accessed 8 January 2014).

to accommodate to their philistinism with extravagant displays of their own subservience.

While the main criteria used in appointing subpanel members and assessors were academic, other considerations also came into play. First, there was an expectation that 'There should be an appropriate degree of continuity in the subpanel's membership from previous assessment exercises', which was secured by requiring one-third of its members to have served in previous RAEs.[51] Whatever its merits, such a stipulation reinforces the risks of intellectual incest that are already inherent in the processes through which panel members and assessors are appointed. Once again we might usefully contrast the National Endowment for the Humanities, which specifically *prohibits* any evaluator from serving in consecutive assessments. Second, HEFCE emphasized the 'desirability of ensuring that the overall body of [panel and subpanel] members reflects the diversity of the research community, including in terms of age, gender, ethnic origin, the scope and focus of their home institution, and geographical location.'[52] HEFCE's own analysis of how far this objective was achieved showed that 'The proportion of female panel members in the REF … is lower than the proportion of females in the permanent academic population' and 'The proportions of some minority ethnic groups and of disabled people in the REF panel membership are generally lower than in the comparator academic staff populations'.[53] Those of us with some sociological training might not find this altogether surprising, given the procedures through which subpanels were constituted. Be that as it may, this diversity requirement – praiseworthy as it may otherwise be – places a further constraint on the composition of panels whose academic competence to judge the range of work submitted to them may already (as I shall shortly argue) be seriously questioned.

Subpanels evaluate UOAs under three headings: Outputs (which count for 65% of the aggregated score), Impact (20%) and Research Environment (15%). Outputs, which will be my main concern here, are judged according to their '"originality, significance and rigour" with reference to international research quality standards'; impact according to its "reach and significance" … [for] the economy, society and/or culture' and the research environment according to its "vitality and sustainability", including its contribution to the

---

[51] *REF 2014: Units of Assessment*, para 55 (e). One third were also required to be new.

[52] *REF 2014: Units of Assessment*, para 56.

[53] *REF 2014: Analysis of Panel Membership*, para 35. On wider REF discrimination against female academics, see Barbara Graziosi, 'Sex and the REF'. *Times Higher Education*, 20 March 2014.

Table 1   Overall quality profile: Definitions of starred levels.[1]

Four star	Quality that is world-leading in terms of originality, significance and rigour.
Three star	Quality that is internationally excellent in terms of originality, significance and rigour but which falls short of the highest standards of excellence.
Two star	Quality that is recognized internationally in terms of originality, significance and rigour.
One star	Quality that is recognized nationally in terms of originality, significance and rigour.
Unclassified	Quality that falls below the standard of nationally recognized work. Or work which does not meet the published definition of research for the purposes of this assessment.

[1]*REF 2014: Assessment framework*, Annex A, 43.

vitality and sustainability of the wider discipline or research base'.[54] Like the boy scouts, each subpanel awards 'stars' within each category. The quality definitions of the starred rankings are as shown in Table 1.

There has been much comment on the imprecision of these definitions, but details of how they are operationalized or benchmarked – beyond relying on the subjective judgements of panel members – have never been published.

At the beginning of the evaluation process, we are told, each 'subpanel chair, consulting with the deputy chair and subpanel members as appropriate, will allocate work to members and assessors with appropriate expertise'. At this stage 'subpanels may recommend the appointment of further additional assessors or, *exceptionally*, request that specific parts of submissions should be cross-referred to another subpanel'.[55] The principles of allocation are nowhere spelled out in HEFCE documentation, but one would expect subpanels to try to strike a balance between ensuring outputs go to the panel member with the most expertise in the field and maintaining some degree of equity of workloads. What actually goes on during panel deliberations is strictly confidential. In the 2008 RAE *all documents showing how subpanels reached their conclusions were shredded and members ordered to destroy personal notes* in order to avoid having to reveal them under Freedom of Information Act requests. One panellist explained, 'It is for our own good. The process could become an absolute nightmare if Departmental Heads or institutions chose to challenge the panels and this information was available'.[56] In any event, HEFCE assures us, 'Each

---

[54]   *REF 2014: Panel Criteria*, para 37. Emphasis added.

[55]   *REF 2014: Panel Criteria*, para 111. Emphasis added.

[56]   Zoe Corbyn, 'Panels ordered to shred all RAE records'. *Times Higher Education*, 17 April 2008.

member and assessor on a subpanel will be allocated a significant volume of material to assess, so that each member and assessor makes a significant contribution to the subpanel's overall recommendations'.[57] 'User assessors' are allocated materials relating to impact only; 'user members' may be given environment templates or even outputs to evaluate where they are willing 'and have appropriate expertise to assess them'.[58]

Each subpanel endeavours to 'develop a common understanding of the quality levels' through 'calibration exercises with respect to outputs and impact … based on samples of a range of outputs' and must 'keep under review the scoring patterns of members and assessors, to ensure consistency in … standards of assessment'. But the REF guidelines are clear that the subpanels 'will *not* make collective judgements about the contributions of individual researchers'.[59] Despite HEFCE's justifications of the process in terms of the subpanels' collective expertise, members and assessors judge the quality of outputs entirely *as individuals*; and in many cases (at least in the humanities) just *one* individual panellist will be responsible for reading and evaluating any particular output. The chair of the History subpanel, Professor Chris Wickham, confirmed this in a briefing talk he gave at several universities during the run-up to the REF.[60] The logistics are such that anything else would probably be impossible within the time frame of the exercise anyway. If one evaluator read each output and workloads were evenly divided between History panel members, each would still have to read and evaluate *at least 250 substantial articles or books*.[61] Any double reading would only add to this burden. Panellists also evaluate environment templates and impact case studies as well as outputs.

Evaluation practices differ across panels, and in disciplines where shorter papers are the normal form of publication multiple readings may be more feasible. Even so, panellists face a huge task. The Physics panel apparently tries to ensure that all outputs are read by at least two members. Peter Coles, Professor of Theoretical Astrophysics and Head of the School of Mathematical

---

[57] *REF 2014: Panel Criteria*, para 114.

[58] *REF 2014: Panel Criteria*, para 115.

[59] *REF 2014: Panel Criteria*, paras 117, 120. Emphasis added.

[60] Professor Wickham spoke at Lancaster University on 23 May 2012.

[61] This is a rough calculation, arrived at by taking the figure for outputs submitted to the History UOA in 2008 REF (6960 outputs, see *REF 2014: Units of Assessment*, Annex B, 13), reducing it by 5% (the fall in the number of staff entered in the humanities in REF 2014) and then dividing it by the number of academic (as distinct from 'user') members and assessors on the REF 2014 History panel (26.5; one assessor is shared with another subpanel).

and Physical Sciences at the University of Sussex, has calculated that this means 'each member of the panel will have to have read 640 research papers. That's an average of about two a day'. He goes on:

> It is therefore blindingly obvious that whatever the panel does do will not be a thorough peer review of each paper, *equivalent to refereeing it for publication in a journal*. The panel members simply won't have the time to do what the REF administrators claim they will do. We will be lucky if they manage a quick skim of each paper before moving on. In other words, it's a sham.[62]

RAE 2008 tried to deal with this problem by allowing panels to determine a minimum proportion of outputs that they would examine in detail, so that they were effectively sampling. These proportions, which were published on the RAE website, ranged from 10% in engineering to 'virtually all' for many social science and humanities panels. It scarcely inspires confidence to read one panellist's admission that: 'You read them sufficiently to form a judgment, to get a feeling … you are using your professional judgment, you don't have to read to the last full stop'.[63] When *Times Higher Education* reported that faced with having to read 'more than a hundred books or papers between February and September' many panellists were 'drowning' under the load, one of them (anonymously) responded:

> your estimates of the scale of work are low in the case of the subject I deal with: not 100 but 1,200 outputs. These are journal articles in the main. It would require at least two or three hours to read each of them properly. Simple arithmetic shows that that is two years' full-time work, while doing nothing else. The evasive notion of 'examining' all outputs and reading 10 per cent (which some engineering subjects have adopted) may lead to situations where some panel members in desperation read nothing at all, on the grounds that the difference between 10 per cent and zero is nugatory and possibly discriminatory. Those individuals would make their judgments entirely on the 100 to 300-word author précis.

The panellist added, 'It is hard to imagine anything like this ever happening again, isn't it?'[64]

---

[62] Peter Coles, 'The apparatus of research assessment is driven by the academic publishing industry and has become entirely self-serving'. LSE Blogs, 14 May 2014, http://blogs.lse.ac.uk/impactofsocialsciences/2013/05/14/the-apparatus-of-research-assessment-is-driven-by-the-academic-publishing-industry/ (accessed 24 February 2014). Emphasis added. Coles assumes 1600 staff members, each submitting four papers, each of which is read by two panel members.

[63] Quoted in Zoe Corbyn, 'Assessors face "drowning" as they endeavour to read 2,363 submissions'. *Times Higher Education*, 17 April 2008.

[64] 'Burning questions for the RAE panels'. *Times Higher Education*, 24 April 2008.

But if anything, the situation got worse with REF 2014. The dependence of the entire process on overworked panellists' personal judgements was now reinforced by specific prohibitions on considering evidence that in other contexts – the North American tenure or promotion proceedings discussed in Chapter 1, for example – would be regarded as highly germane to research evaluation. This is a direct result of HEFCE's U-turn on metrics. While panels can make limited use of 'additional information', they are warned: 'No subpanel may make use of journal impact factors, rankings or lists, or the perceived standing of the publisher, in assessing the quality of research outputs'.[65] Those panels that are permitted to use citation data may do so *only* to provide 'additional information about the academic significance of submitted outputs'; moreover, they are instructed to 'recognise the limited value of citation data for recently published outputs, the variable citation patterns for different fields of research, the possibility of "negative citations", and the limitations of such data for outputs in languages other than English'.[66] Panel C disciplines (economics aside) do not use citations,[67] and Panel D categorically states that none of its subpanels 'will … receive nor make use of any citation or bibliometric data to inform their judgements'.[68] Universities were also discouraged from relying on citations 'to inform the selection of staff or outputs for inclusion in their submissions'.[69]

There is a good deal of anecdotal evidence to suggest that despite these strictures, bibliometric data were widely used by individual universities to select both staff and outputs for submission in REF 2014.[70] Peter Coles claims that the physics panel used citations as a proxy for quality (when it wasn't supposed to) in RAE 2008 and will have no realistic alternative but to do the same in REF 2014. 'If you look at the volume of work facing the REF panel members', he argues, 'it's pretty clear that citation statistics will be much more important … than we've been led to believe. The panel simply won't have the time or the breadth of understanding to do an in-depth assessment of every paper, so will inevitably in many cases be led by bibliometric information'. Such covert recourse to bibliometrics, he believes, will do far more harm than if they had been transparently employed with proper critical attention being paid to the

---

[65] *REF 2014: Panel Criteria*, para 53. Emphasis added.

[66] *REF 2014: Panel Criteria*, para 51.

[67] *REF 2014: Panel Criteria*, Part 2 (C), para 64. For economics, see paras 65–67.

[68] *REF 2014: Panel Criteria*, Part 2(D), para 74.

[69] *REF 2014: Panel Criteria*, para 52.

[70] See Jenny Rohn, 'Business as usual in judging the worth of a researcher?' *Guardian*, Occam's Corner, 30 November 2012, and the UCU surveys discussed below, pp. 75–8.

limitations of particular measures and sources. He notes that Elsevier's SCOPUS service, from which HEFCE provides citation data to panels as 'additional information', does not cover the open access arXiv repository of 907,086 e-prints in physics, mathematics, computer science, quantitative biology, quantitative finance and statistics.[71] Nevertheless HEFCE's intention to press on regardless is plain. *'Expert review of the outputs'*, it thunders as it rides into the valley of Death, *'will remain the primary means of assessing them'*.[72]

2.3 EVALUATING OUTPUTS: 'AN APPROPRIATE BREADTH OF RESEARCH EXPERTISE'?

If individual REF panellists' personal judgements play such a critical part in appraisals of outputs, then the least that can be asked is that – in the words of HEFCE's guidelines – 'The subpanel members and additional assessors should provide *sufficient breadth and depth of expertise* to undertake the assessment *across the subpanel's remit* (including as appropriate expertise in interdisciplinary research and expertise in the wider use or benefits of research)'.[73] Not only does REF 2014 lamentably fail to satisfy this requirement, there was no way in which it could ever have hoped to do so. This is not just a matter of this or that area of research not being adequately covered by this or that subpanel. The problems go much deeper. At issue is what constitutes peer review.

It is a curiosity, to begin with, that an exercise that purports to evaluate the 'originality, significance and rigour' of outputs 'with reference to international research quality standards' should leave their appraisal wholly in the hands of people based in British universities (and predominantly of older, male, white people based in British universities at that).[74] Unless we make the ludicrous (though not uncharacteristically older, male and white British) assumption that UK-based academics are top of the class in everything they do, this must mean that in at least some areas the REF is denying itself the opportunity of making use of the best international expertise available. The hubris involved here is all the more striking in that REF *defines* the quality of research *entirely in terms of its international reputation* – with 4* research being 'world-leading', 3* 'internationally excellent' and 2* 'internationally recognised'.[75] Research that is only

---

[71] Coles, 'The apparatus of research assessment'.

[72] *REF 2014: Panel Criteria*, para 121. Emphasis added.

[73] *REF 2014: Units of Assessment*, para 55 (b). Emphasis added.

[74] See *REF 2014: Analysis of Panel Membership* for a detailed breakdown.

[75] *REF 2014: Panel Criteria*, para 37. Emphasis added.

'nationally recognised' gets the lowest grade of 1*, yet HEFCE sees no inconsistency in recruiting the people who will make these judgements of relative international standing from a single national pool.

The Roberts report on the 2001 RAE recommended maintaining 'dependence upon expert peer review to identify the best research' as evaluated by 'panel members recruited from within the research community', but added the important rider: '*but not necessarily all UK-based academics*'.[76] Two articles published by way of an obituary for the RAE in *Times Higher Education* on 30 November 2007 shed further light on this perennial problem. 'International assessments are still being made by national assessors, first and foremost', complained Alex Danchev, then Professor of International Relations at Nottingham University, who questioned whether 'international recognition is ... the self-evident proposition it is sometimes made to seem. International excellence is properly *comparative*. Is the RAE', he asked, 'well designed to make such judgments?'[77] David Eastwood (who sat on the Roberts review) went further, conceding that 'international benchmarking of quality' was 'one thing that the RAE has not been able to do' – which might be thought a trifle odd, given that the scale used to evaluate each and every research output in RAE 2008 claimed to distinguish degrees of international excellence. Eastwood still had hopes then that the REF would solve the problem with 'bibliometrics, used with sensitivity and sophistication',[78] but we know where that proposal ended up. The only acknowledgement in REF 2014 that appraisal 'with reference to international quality standards' might benefit from involving the occasional foreigner is the presence of international members on Main Panels, who are supposed to ensure that 'subpanels adhere to internationally referenced standards'.[79] They are in a small minority, especially in the social sciences (4/22) and humanities (4/20), and it is hard to see how significant an input or effective an oversight they can have.[80] Like much else in the REF their main function appears to be window-dressing.

One might, I suppose, attempt to justify this idiosyncrasy by pointing to the UK's disproportionate international excellence in research. The

---

[76] *Review of research assessment: Report by Sir Gareth Roberts*, 6. Emphasis added.

[77] Alex Danchev, 'Goodbye to the RAE ... and hello to the REF'. *Times Higher Education*, 30 November 2007. Emphasis added.

[78] David Eastwood, 'Goodbye to the RAE ... and hello to the REF'. *Times Higher Education*, 30 November 2007.

[79] *REF 2014: Units of Assessment*, para 33.

[80] Here and below I draw on *REF 2014: Panel Membership Lists (updated December 2013)*. http://www.ref.ac.uk/panels/panelmembership/ (accessed 13 January 2013).

Department of Business, Innovation and Skills (DBIS), under whose aegis UK universities currently fall, boasts that 'while the UK represents just 0.9% of global population, 3.2% of R&D expenditure, and 4.1% of researchers, it accounts for 9.5% of downloads, 11.6% of citations and 15.9% of the world's most highly-cited articles'.[81] Like the Russell Group in other contexts, DBIS has no qualms about using citation data as an indicator of the 'international comparative performance of the UK research base', maintaining that 'Normalised citation impact *does* correlate with other assessments of research quality ... and so it can be seen as a good indicator of research performance – especially for larger samples'.[82] But – to give these numbers a somewhat different spin – while 95.9% of researchers, 90.5% of downloads, 88.4% of citations and 84.1% of the world's most highly-cited articles do *not* hail from Britain's universities, almost 100% of REF evaluators do. The academic members and assessors on the subpanels – *the people who actually do all the reading and scoring of outputs* – work in UK institutions unless they moved abroad after they were appointed. Graeme Rosenberg responded to criticisms that a subpanel chair who had moved to Sciences-Po in Paris after appointment would not be able to do his job properly by observing: 'We have a number of people on the panels from overseas or with overseas experience or interests. This is a distinct advantage as the panels are, after all, judging work against international standards'.[83] Quite.

I imagine that it was costs and logistics rather than post-imperial hubris that led HEFCE to assume that assessors drawn from UK universities alone would suffice to evaluate close to 200,000 individual research outputs against international standards, but the presumption – in all senses – is gargantuan. No doubt it says something about British elites' perceptions of their own superiority. Not only does REF practice in this respect starkly conflict with peer review in academic journal and book publishing, where reviewers are sought on the basis of their knowledge of the field irrespective of their national affiliation, but it deviates equally sharply from peer review in research grant competitions, where funding agencies also use disciplinary panels to decide on awards. The key difference with the REF is that although members of such panels may be drawn from a single national university system, their judgements are informed by external appraisals from all over the world. Canada's SSHRC – of which I have

---

[81] *International Comparative Performance of the UK Research Base – 2013*. A report prepared by Elsevier for the UK's Department of Business, Innovation and Skills (BIS), 2.

[82] *International Comparative Performance of the UK Research Base*, 7. Emphasis added.

[83] Quoted in Paul Jump, 'Paris post will not weaken panellist's "duty" to REF'. *Times Higher Education*, 28 March 2013.

had experience as an applicant, a three-time grant-holder, an expert reviewer and a panellist[84] – uses 'appropriate expert reviewers to assess the individual merit of all proposals against the published criteria' who 'are enlisted based on individual experience and expertise, and ... may be from Canada or abroad'.[85] But it *separates* 'the merit review of proposals ... from the making of funding decisions. Those acting as reviewers will not also be responsible for authorizing the funding decision', which is made by disciplinary panels that score and rank all applications.[86] In tenure and promotion proceedings – including in many British universities – it is often obligatory for a file to be sent to international referees, especially at senior levels.

This is not the only problem with the composition of REF panels. We saw earlier that reducing RAE 2008's 67 subpanels to REF 2014's 36 led some to question their ability to provide adequate coverage of the fields that came under their remit. The slimming down of the panels merely highlights a more general problem. No subpanel small enough to be capable of working effectively is likely to contain the necessary 'breadth and depth of expertise' to provide equally informed assessment across all the sub-fields of any academic discipline (let alone interdisciplinary work, as REF 2014 now requires); and this inequity in turn casts doubts on the REF's ability to deliver judgements that are either competent or fair. Let me take the history panel, whose remit has not changed since RAE 2008, as an example. The panel has a chair, a deputy chair and 23 members, of whom three are 'user members' representing the Wellcome Trust, Minerva Media and Historic Royal Palaces.[87] There are a further 14 assessors, 9 of whom are research

---

[84] I have held SSHRC grants from the History, Sociology and Interdisciplinary Studies committees and acted as a reviewer for all three. I served as a member of SSHRC's disciplinary panel for anthropology, sociology and cognate disciplines in the 2013–2014 postdoctoral fellowships competition.

[85] SSHRC, 'Merit Review'. http://www.sshrc-crsh.gc.ca/funding-financement/ merit_review-evaluation_du_merite/index-eng.aspx (accessed 18 January 2014).

[86] SSHRC, 'Principles for Merit Review'. http://www.sshrc-crsh.gc.ca/funding-financement/merit_review-evaluation_du_merite/index-eng.aspx (accessed 18 January 2014). More than one panel member reads each proposal, and where there is a significant discrepancy between scores, the case will be discussed and, if necessary, voted on by the entire panel. See *SSHRC Manual For Adjudication Committee Members 2013–2014*. http://www.sshrc-crsh.gc.ca/funding-financement/ merit_review-evaluation_du_merite/adjudication_manual_2013-guide_ membres_2013-eng.pdf (accessed 18 January 2014).

[87] 'Main Panel D Membership (December 2013)'. http://www.ref.ac.uk/panels/ panelmembership/ (accessed 13 January 2013).

users (and therefore not eligible to evaluate outputs).[88] The 27 academic members and assessors on the panel have to read close to 7000 outputs from over 1750 researchers, potentially covering all periods of history and areas of the world.[89]

Attempts have clearly been made to achieve various kinds of balance, though it is not always an especially equitable one. There are 16 men and 11 women[90] among the evaluators on a panel that (so far as I can tell) is uniformly white. Universities from all parts of the UK are represented, with only four having more than one panel member or assessor and none more than two. Nineteen evaluators hail from Russell Group universities, a further six from the 1994 Group and only two from institutions out-side the magic circle (the Universities of Keele and Hertfordshire). The coverage of medieval (3), early modern (5)[91] and modern history (19) is probably a fair reflection of the chronological distribution of the outputs to be assessed. This may also be the rationale for the skewed – and decid-edly limited – geographic range of the panel's expertise. Twelve panellists and four assessors are historians of Britain;[92] of these, three also work in imperial history.[93] There are six historians of various European countries, two historians of the United States and one of Africa (which thus gets the same coverage as Wales, which may or may not say something about the

---

[88] The five academic assessors were added in June 2013, probably in the interest of covering gaps in coverage or relieving workload. I exclude user member/assessors in the calculations that follow, since my major concern is with the panel's range of academic expertise.

[89] Based on figures for 2008 RAE submissions given in *REF 2014: Units of Assessment*, Annex B, 13. The actual figure for outputs might be lower in practice due to double weighting of books, but this scarcely eases the task of evaluation since in most cases the length of a history book amounts to many times more than twice that of an article.

[90] Sharon Montieth (Nottingham University) is jointly appointed to Sub-panel 29, English Language and Literature.

[91] I include in the early modern count one intellectual historian (Colin Kidd, St Andrew's) whose interests span the periods historians distinguish as 'early modern' (16th–18th centuries) and 'modern' (later 18th century onwards). In characterizing panellists' research expertise I have drawn on their pages on university websites.

[92] I include here Chris Williams (Cardiff), a historian of Wales, and Keith Jeffery (Queen's University, Belfast), some of whose work deals with Ireland (at a time when it was ruled from Britain).

[93] Margot Finn (UCL; India), Clare Anderson (Leicester; India/South Asia) and Keith Jeffery.

horizons of history as a discipline in the UK).[94] Two panellists define their expertise thematically rather than geographically.[95] Nobody appears to have specialist knowledge of Spain, Portugal, Central and Eastern Europe (apart from Russia), the Middle East, Latin America, Australasia, China, Japan or anywhere else in Asia except where that continent's long and eventful history had the good or bad fortune to intersect with that of imperial Britain. There is a decent spread of sub-fields across economic, social, political, cultural, military, religious and intellectual history, while non-traditional areas such as gender, consumption, emotions and the body are also represented.

Whether this hodgepodge amounts to 'an *appropriate* breadth of research expertise' to judge the originality, significance and rigour of *every* submitted history output from *every* university in the UK – which is what, after all, the panel is supposed to provide – is questionable. I myself rather doubt it, but then I am not the 'community' whose confidence HEFCE claims REF panels command. What is *not* debatable is that the chances of outputs in history being read by panellists who are experts in an author's field are very unevenly distributed. Structuring the panel to give the evaluators comparable work-loads may make organizational sense but it creates serious inequities for those whose research is being assessed. The odds of a modern historian's outputs finding their way to an evaluator who is familiar not only with his or her period, but also with the same country and maybe even the same research area are a good deal higher than for early modernists or medievalists simply because there is a wider spread of modernists on the panel. For the same reason historians of Britain are much more likely to find a reader who works on the same period or in the same field than historians of Germany, France, Russia or Holland (each of which have one representative on the panel). The REF may claim to assess 'all types of research and all forms of research output ... *on a fair and equal basis*',[96] but in this context some histories are more equal than others.

---

[94] Paul Nugent (Edinburgh). Though Nugent has pan-African interests and is joint editor of the *Journal of Modern African Studies* and president at AEGIS – African Studies in Europe, his personal expertise is Ghana, Togo, Senegal, Gambia and South Africa. I imagine asking him to evaluate an article on, say, Egypt, would make as much sense as asking a Swedish historian to appraise an article on Montenegro. See http://uk.linkedin.com/pub/paul-nugent/21/8b9/62b (accessed 13 January 2014).

[95] Catherine Schenk (Glasgow), an economic historian who has done work on Hong Kong; John Young (Nottingham), a historian of foreign policy who has worked on the UK, US and EU.

[96] *REF 2014: Panel Criteria*, para 40. Emphasis added.

Let us suppose that a paper titled 'Religious Sects in Seventeenth-Century Russia: A Revisionist Interpretation' is submitted to the History panel. Who should read it: the panel's lone Russian historian (whose period is the 20th century and whose field is political history)? One of its five early modernists (none of whom specialize in either Russian history or religion)? Its only ecclesiastical historian (whose area of research is early medieval England)? None are ideal readers, because none are experts *in the field to which the paper contributes*. I would insist that none – to return to the REF assessment criteria – are qualified to assess its *originality* or *significance*, since such judgements by definition demand knowledge of the current state of that field. None would figure on any journal editor's list of appropriate reviewers for our hypothetical article. Nor would any be likely to be invited to provide specialist assessments of a proposal on such a topic in grant competitions (though they might well serve on an AHRC or ESRC adjudicating panel), or be nominated as suitable external referees in a tenure or promotion case for an author in this field. This is not because they lack eminence in the historical profession, but because they do not have – in HEFCE's words – 'the expertise to reach robust and fair judgments *with regard to the submitted material*'.[97] Professional eminence and specialist expertise are two different things, and the one does not always entail the other.

Should all papers on American history, then, be divided up between the panel's two US historians? To do so at least guarantees a reading by somebody with expertise on the country, if not necessarily on the period and not likely in the field. But it also raises the spectre of gatekeeping. Does the academic community *really* want all outputs submitted to the REF on American history to be judged by just two people? Taking the point further, should everything on Russian history be appraised by the one Russian specialist on the panel, everything on Germany by the one German specialist – and everything on the entire continent of Africa evaluated by the one African historian? To do so is to grant these individuals' opinions extraordinary weight in a context in which the financial and reputational stakes are unusually high. Again, standard peer review procedures are designed to avoid this dilemma by soliciting multiple appraisals. But the only alternative within the REF framework is to trust other members of the panel to make the fine distinctions between 2*, 3* and 4* contributions to fields that are not their specialties. The *reductio ad absurdum* comes with the history of China, Turkey or Brazil, or – as in the case of my own research – the Czech Lands, where there is nobody on the

---

[97] *REF 2014: Panel Criteria*, para 31. Emphasis added.

panel 'with appropriate expertise' (or possibly any knowledge at all). They don't know the languages, they don't know the archives, they don't know the sources and they don't know the secondary literature. On what possible basis can they determine whether an output in these fields is 'internationally excellent' or merely 'internationally recognized' – the crucial boundary between 3* and 2* – especially when they are expressly forbidden to use any bibliometric or other contextual data? Whatever the panel decides to do in such cases, by no stretch of the imagination can it be described as expert review.

History may be extreme in its diversity of chronological range, geographic span, substantive foci and methodological orientations (which may differ in their conceptions of 'rigour') but comparable issues must arise to a greater or lesser extent within every disciplinary subpanel. Earlier I quoted Peter Coles's doubts that the physics panel has sufficient 'breadth of understanding to do an in-depth assessment of every paper'. The underlying problem here is not the panels' composition per se. Composition becomes a problem only because the REF process *does all evaluation of outputs in-house*, refusing to solicit any external specialist advice; in some panels, *relies on a single panel member to evaluate each output*; and *disregards any and all external indicators*, including venue of publication, citations and book reviews. I am not denying the problems with bibliometric data, which opponents of metrics have rehearsed ad nauseam. But wilfully ignoring all consideration of whether an output has gone through a prior process of peer review, where it has been published, how it has been received and how often and by whom it has been cited in favour of the subjective opinion of just one evaluator who may have no expertise in the field does not seem to me a very defensible alternative. It also gives extraordinary gatekeeping power to the individuals on the REF subpanels.

Any one of these factors would seriously undermine the credibility of appraisals in any of the peer reviewing contexts – publication, grant funding, tenure and promotion decisions – examined in Chapter 1. Taken together they devastate it. The feature of the REF in which HEFCE takes most pride – its 'expert review of the outputs' – turns out to be exactly what its procedures are incapable of delivering in any reliable or consistent way. The truth of the matter is that the panels are a crapshoot and the appraisals a farce. Stevan Harnad and I may have had our disagreements over Open Access publication, but he went to the heart of what is wrong with the UK's research assessment system when (writing of the 2008 RAE) he stated bluntly *'that was not "peer review" in any case*; peer review is done by journal referees, selected among the world's top experts, in the case of the best journals, not from a single country's rag-tag generic panel'.[98] Small wonder that every research university in the land was desperate to get its people on to REF panels.

2.4 THE RUSSELL GROUP, QR FUNDING AND INSTITUTIONAL GAMING

The precise funding formula that determines how the scores awarded for each UOA in REF 2014 will translate into cash for individual universities over the next five or six years is yet to be announced, but the general principles are clear. Government channels its support for university research through the 'dual system'. The larger share of the budget goes to the research councils, which annually invest around £3bn across all academic disciplines.[99] These investments mainly take the form of research grants and PhD studentships and need not concern us here. HEFCE and the other funding councils provide 'block grant funding for institutions to support the research infrastructure and enable ground-breaking research in keeping with their own mission'.[100] This is the QR funding discussed earlier. Unlike research council funding, which is tied to projects and studentships, universities can spend QR income as they see fit. It is allocated on the basis of *volume* of research (measured by the number of research-active staff entered in the RAE/REF), *costs* of research (laboratory-based subjects have a higher weighting) and *quality* of research as measured by RAE/REF performance. RAE 2008 gave each UOA a 'profile' showing the proportion of outputs that fell into each of the starred quality bands rather than an aggregate score as previously.[101] The relation between these profiles and the income a university would receive in HEFCE research support was made crystal clear in the QR funding formula announced in January 2009, which weighted outputs on a scale

---

[98] Stevan Harnad, 'Citations ideas 1'. *Times Higher Education*, 4 January 2008. For my disagreements with Professor Harnad on Open Access see http://coastsofbohemia.com/2013/03/04/more-on-open-access-hefce-brings-out-the-big-ref-stick/ and http://coastsofbohemia.com/2013/03/07/april-fools-day-rcuk-adds-fuel-to-the-open-access-fire/ (posted 4 and 7 March 2013, respectively).

[99] Research Council UK (RCUK) home page. http://www.rcuk.ac.uk/Pages/Home.aspx (accessed 16 January 2013).

[100] HEFCE, 'How we fund research'. http://www.hefce.ac.uk/whatwedo/rsrch/howfundr/ (accessed 16 January 2014).

[101] HEFCE, *Securing world-class research in UK universities: Exploring the impact of block grant funding* [nd], 17. http://www.hefce.ac.uk/research/funding/resfund/QR.pdf http://www.universitiesuk.ac.uk/highereducation/Pages/WorldClassResearch.aspx#.U1VUm8bwDDE

of 1* = 0, 2* = 1, 3* = 3, and 4* = 7. A 4* output would give a university seven times whatever a 2* output was worth when the numbers were crunched.[102]

The amount of QR funding HEFCE disburses each year varies according to how much money it receives from the public purse and how it chooses to divide this up between support for teaching, research or other activities.[103] In 2012–2013 HEFCE distributed £1050m in mainstream QR funds.[104] While this figure is barely a third of the funding available through RCUK, it is a significant element in leading universities' budgets, not least because it is heavily concentrated in the top schools. 'QR funding has always been highly selective, targeted at areas where there is evidence of the highest quality', HEFCE explains, adding, 'The new profiles from the 2008 RAE enabled funding bodies to target funding in a more fine-grained way, rewarding excellence wherever it was found'.[105] The intention was that the profiles would help identify and enable support for emergent as well as established areas of strength. The Russell Group, however, attacked the 'wider dispersal of funding across the sector' that resulted from RAE 2008, complaining that its 'percentage share of total recurrent research funding in England declined from 65 per cent (in 2008-09) to 62 per cent, and ... accounted for only 23 per cent of the overall uplift in HEFCE recurrent research funding in 2009-10'. This 'reduction in concentration of research funding', it warned, 'risks damaging the UK's research base and compromising the sustainability of our leading universities'.[106] The government began to lean on HEFCE to force further concentration shortly thereafter.

Following an instruction from DBIS late in 2010 that only 'internationally excellent research' should henceforth qualify for QR support, HEFCE slashed the weighting of 2* outputs from 1.0 to 0.294 in 2011–2012, redistributing some of the money to increase the amount paid to universities per 3* and 4* item. At

---

[102] For a fuller account see HEFCE, 'The QR Funding Formula' [nd], http://www.hefcw. ac.uk/documents/policy_areas/research/qr%20funding%20method.pdf (accessed 18 January 2014). A step-to-step guide to how overall quality profiles (which include rankings for impact and environment as well as outputs) are arrived at in REF 2014 is provided in *REF 2014: Assessment framework*, Annex B.

[103] HEFCE, 'Mainstream QR Funding'. http://www.hefce.ac.uk/whatwedo/rsrch/ howfundr/mainstreamqr/ (accessed 16 January 2014).

[104] HEFCE, 'Funding for universities and colleges for 2012-13: Board decisions'. Circular letter, 1 February 2012. http://www.hefce.ac.uk/pubs/ (accessed 16 January 2013).

[105] *Securing world-class research in UK universities*, 17.

[106] The Russell Group of Universities, *The concentration of research funding in the UK: driving excellence and competing globally* (Autumn 2009). http://www.russellgroup. ac.uk/Policies-Research-funding/ (accessed 17 January 2014).

the same time the relative weight of a 4* output was increased from 7 to 9. The justification for these changes was made explicit:

> The Board decided, *in response to the Government's presumption* … in favour of more research concentration, to introduce a steeper funding 'slope' for all subjects by increasing the weightings for work at different levels … The effect of the change will provide *an initial step towards increased concentration* …[107]

The following year HEFCE removed all remaining funding for 2* outputs. Since 'over 60 per cent of staff in 4* departments in the 2008 RAE were in Russell Group universities and, on average, twice as much of the research undertaken at Russell Group universities was 4* rated than in the rest of the sector',[108] the Matthew principle triumphed. By 2012–2013 the Russell Group's share of QR funding had increased by almost ten percentage points to 71.7%, with the largest single amount – £132m – going to the University of Oxford.[109] A further 12.5% went to the 1994 Group universities.

My concern here is not with the policy of concentrating research funding as such, a principle I would support, albeit with reservations.[110] It is with the consequences that the method used to achieve this – the changes to the QR funding formula – had for the 2014 REF. So long as 2* outputs – which formed the largest single category in most universities' submissions in the 2008 RAE – had some financial value, institutions had to weigh up the costs and benefits of entering the maximum number of research-active staff (and thus maximizing QR income) against attempting to select for quality (which would enhance standings in the league table). Some schools may have been more 'strategic' than others in making this choice.[111] Examining such evidence as

---

[107] HEFCE, 'Funding for universities and colleges in 2010-11' (Circular Letter February 2010), para 25. http://www.hefce.ac.uk/pubs/year/2010/cl022010/name,62741,en.html (accessed 16 January 2014). Emphasis added.

[108] Russell Group, *Concentration of Research Funding*, 4.

[109] Paul Jump, 'Elite Powers of Concentration'. *Times Higher Education*, 20 March 2012.

[110] The benefits of 'critical mass' seem to me to be undeniable whether we are talking of staff, research students, facilities and equipment, or library resources. I also accept the comparison made by the Russell Group with the United States, where there is an explicit hierarchy of institutions with only a minority (614, or just under 9% of 7018 institutions) offering PhD programs (*Concentration of Research Funding*, 6).

[111] Several universities made their RAE 2008 staff submission rates public. See 'Lancaster produces alternative RAE 2008 rankings'. *Times Higher Education*, 18 December 2008. A number of post-1992 universities admitted to being highly selective, while Warwick University was accused by the UCU of excluding up to 25% of staff in some departments. See Zoe Corbyn, 'Exclusions from RAE see steep rise'. *Times Higher Education*, 2 November 2007.

was available[112] after the total numbers submitted to RAE 2008 were published, *Times Higher Education* reported 'a strong trend among teaching-led universities to exclude more staff from the 2008 RAE than in 2001, while the figure from research-intensive universities appeared not to vary dramatically'.[113] Most research universities seem to have submitted most of their eligible staff and their websites boasted of the high proportions of their faculty that were research active as indexed by submission in the RAE. But the combination of steepening the curve (so that by 2012–2013 a 4* output was worth three times as much as a 3* output) and defunding 2* outputs (so that there was now no difference in financial reward to a university between 2*, 1* and unclassified outputs) threatened to turn the REF into even more of gaming process than any previous RAE had been.

In the words of Adam Tickell, Pro Vice-Chancellor for Research and Knowledge Transfer at the University of Birmingham, universities had 'no rational reason to submit people who haven't got at least one 3* piece of work'[114] to REF 2014. He expanded on this at a Higher Education Policy Institute conference in November 2013, explaining that 'the removal in 2011 of funding for work rated 2* meant that half the work Birmingham submitted to the 2008 research assessment exercise was not funded – something the institution had taken as a "serious wake-up call"'.[115] In the 2014 REF, unlike the 2008 RAE, *any* outputs scored below 3* dilute a university's ranking relative to competitors without any compensating gain in income. The last thing any institution that aspires to be seen as a research university wants is for the GPA that would be achieved by its 3* and 4* outputs to be reduced by a long 'tail' of 2* evaluations. Given the low financial return to 3* as compared with 4* outputs, there is also little to be gained (and much to be risked) from entering any staff

---

[112] No data were published that allowed any systematic comparisons of numbers of staff submitted and numbers eligible to be submitted at university or UOA level. Such data will be published (we are promised) for REF 2014. See Paul Jump, 'REF "contextual data" decision could enrich league tables'. *Times Higher Education*, 3 December 2013.

[113] Zoe Corbyn, 'Number of staff entered for RAE rises by 12%'. *Times Higher Education*, 31 January 2008. The total number of staff whose research was submitted rose by 12% on RAE 2001, but it is not possible to draw direct inferences on selectivity.

[114] Quoted in Paul Jump, 'Research intelligence – What's on the cards for the REF?' *Times Higher Education*, 20 September 2012.

[115] Quoted in Paul Jump, 'Cherry-pick submissions or risk picking up REF tab'. *Times Higher Education*, 21 November 2013. Some participants drew the opposite conclusion: Jump reports that David Price, Vice-Provost for Research at University College London, called for future REFs 'to include a metrics-based assessment of all outputs produced by all academics within the assessment period'.

member in the REF who does not have a *safe* majority of 3* outputs in his or her portfolio. In order to maximize the returns from the REF, the rational strategy for every research university is to exclude outputs likely to achieve a ranking of 2* or below from entering its submission, even if this means that fewer faculty are entered in the REF. The problem is how to ensure this – since there is no reliable way of predicting how REF subpanels will grade the individual outputs submitted to them, given the extreme subjectivity of the process.

Universities responded differently to these pressures (and many were, and have remained, less than forthcoming about their REF staff selection practices). But it was widely expected that research universities would be more selective in who they submitted than in RAE 2008. Some made this intention explicit. Lancaster University responded to other institutions' suspected gaming in 2008 by publishing an 'alternative' RAE league table that endeavoured to 'correct' for selectivity.[116] But it posted a statement on its internal staff website early in 2013 warning that:

> Lancaster University is aiming to maximise its ranking in each UoA submission so final decisions will be based on the most advantageous overall profile for the University. It is anticipated that the number of staff submitted to REF2014 will be below the 92% submitted for RAE2008 and not all contractually REF-eligible staff will be submitted.[117]

Lancaster was not alone in embarking on this course of action. *Times Higher Education* submitted a Freedom of Information Act request to all 126 UK universities late in 2012 asking what their 'GPA' would be for selecting staff for submission to REF 2014. Fourteen did not respond and four sent 'uninformative responses'. Twenty refused to reveal their figure, 'mostly on the grounds that disclosure would be likely to prejudice their "commercial interests"'. Fifteen universities were not at that point planning to impose any thresholds, 11 planned variable thresholds and 32 had not yet made up their minds. Thirty universities had already decided on their GPA cut-offs, of which 12 required a majority of work to be rated 3* or higher.[118]

Looking forward to the REF in November 2007, David Eastwood had assured universities that HEFCE was 'as committed to lightening the burden as

---

[116] 'Lancaster produces alternative RAE 2008 rankings'. The basis for its calculations was the 'contextual data' estimating eligible staff numbers provided in *Times Higher Education* league tables.

[117] 'REF Statement'. http://www.lancaster.ac.uk/depts/research/lancaster/REF2014.html (accessed 17 January 2014).

[118] Paul Jump, 'Research intelligence – What's on the cards for the REF?'

we are to rigour in assessing quality, so identifying excellence will remain both a mantra and reality'.[119] In the event he got neither. I have already demonstrated that REF panels' ability to identify excellence is more than questionable. As for 'lightening the burden', not only did the REF require universities to produce new (and extensive) data on impact that had not been sought in any previous RAE, but HEFCE's changes to the QR funding formula in 2010–2011 also led universities to institute internal assessments of the quality of outputs *before* they were submitted for the REF in order to screen out likely low-scoring items. Many mounted their own full-scale 'mock-REF' exercises, in Lancaster's case two years before the real thing. Whatever the REF's 'new system' offered, it was not the 'lighter touch' and 'reduced burden' that Eastwood had promised.[120] The time and resources swallowed up by such local assessments – not to mention the increased stress they put on the staff members who were now being internally as well as externally evaluated – were huge.

When *Times Higher Education* asked university Heads of research in February 2014 how the REF experience had been for them, none agreed

> that the revised process was any less labour-intensive than the last RAE in 2008 ... One says it was at least as onerous [and] the others say it was more so. One estimates the required workload to have been three or four times greater.

The burden of having to prepare impact case studies (which Barbara Pittam, director of academic services at the Institute of Cancer Research, likened to 'writing up a PhD thesis with 20 supervisors') was an important element in this increased workload, as was the bureaucracy surrounding documentation of special circumstances like pregnancy, sickness or disability. But several research Heads also acknowledged that: 'one reason for the increased workload in the REF was the need to establish robust mechanisms for assessing the quality of research produced by staff'. While HEFCE predicts that REF 2014 will cost universities broadly the same (£47m) as RAE 2008, one respondent insisted that an 'honest assessment' would be nearer to £200m. 'The amount of valuable research that this could have funded is immense [and the results are] unlikely to tell us anything significant that we don't know already', he complained.[121]

But the issue here is not just one of workloads and costs. With this 'need to establish robust mechanisms for assessing the quality of research produced by staff' the whole character of the UK's national research assessment exercises

---

[119] Eastwood, 'Goodbye to the RAE ...'

[120] Eastwood, 'Goodbye to the RAE ...'

[121] Paul Jump, 'The REF: how was it for you?' *Times Higher Education*, 27 February 2014.

changed. The uniform and relatively transparent – if far from expert – processes for evaluating outputs through RAE panels that had been a hallmark of the system since 1992 were now supplemented (and for those who were excluded, usurped) by the highly divergent, frequently ad hoc and generally anything but transparent staff selection procedures of individual universities. It is a reasonable presumption that most research universities did their best to enter most of their research-active scholars in the 2008 RAE, though there seem also to have been some notable exceptions. But in the 2014 REF key decisions on quality of outputs were taken *within the individual university*, with *no significant external scrutiny* (and often no meaningful internal public discussion), *before these outputs could enter the official national evaluative process at all*. Robust is the last adjective that should be applied to such procedures, unless it is intended to bring to mind the physiognomy of bouncers, goons and enforcers. If the REF evaluation process is flawed when measured against the international norms of peer review discussed in Chapter 1, it is a model of rigour, transparency and fairness compared with staff selection processes at university level. This largely hidden underbelly of the REF forms the subject of the next chapter.

3

DOWN AND DIRTY

3.1 THE KAFKAN WORLD OF LANCASTER HISTORY: A CASE STUDY

The funding councils required every university 'to develop, document and apply a code of practice on selecting staff to include in their REF submissions'.[1] Nobody wanted to repeat the experience of RAE 2008, when 'many institutions produced Codes of Practice that did little more than meet minimum standards, and ... were not communicated widely or applied effectively'.[2] HEFCE asked universities to submit their draft codes for prior vetting by its Equality and Diversity Advisory Panel before 31 July 2012. It says a lot that out of 159 codes the panel examined,

> Nearly half ... fell short of meeting some aspect of the guidance ... The most common areas where the Codes tended to fall short ... were in lacking detail about how the Code would be communicated to all staff, or not clearly setting out timely and independent appeals processes.

Where codes were deficient, 'the relevant Funding Body ... corresponded directly with the institution concerned'.[3] HEFCE encouraged universities to 'continue to reflect on their practices, and the effects of these, as they implement their Codes during the coming months', stressing: 'It is essential that the rigorous standards and processes outlined in the Codes *are fully implemented*

---

[1] *REF 2014: Assessment framework*, para 188.

[2] HEFCE, *Research excellence framework: Codes of Practice on the selection of staff. A report on good practice by the Equality and Diversity Advisory Panel (EDAP)* (October 2012), 2. http://www.ref.ac.uk/pubs/ (accessed 20 January 2014).

[3] *Codes of Practice on the selection of staff*, 2.

in practice as selection decisions are made'.[4] Indeed, it suggested, 'Institutions that conduct mock REF exercises might consider using them as an opportunity to apply their draft code and refine it further'.[5]

Lancaster University's Code of Practice promised 'to ensure transparency and fairness in the decision making process within the University over the selection of eligible staff for submission into the REF'.[6] It is long on promises and short on specifics, with all the wriggle-room one expects of such documents. Implausibly, given all the other important things VCs have to do, the code claims that 'all selection decisions regarding the University submission to the REF will lie with the Vice-Chancellor on the advice of the REFSG [REF Steering Group]. No other group will be *formally* involved in the selection of staff to be returned'.[7] So far as I can see, what this does is to limit any legal liability for selection to the VC and a senior advisory committee while protecting those involved in the actual assessment of outputs at departmental and faculty level against potential litigation. It is these latter evaluations, however, that provided the basis upon which the REFSG and VC actually made their decisions. We are assured that REFSG will 'develop open and transparent selection criteria', 'detail the communication channels to be used to convey the relevant information', 'detail an appeal process that can be used by all members of eligible staff in order to seek further consideration for submission' and 'ensure that selection for REF submissions do not discriminate on the grounds of age, disability, gender reassignment, marriage and civil partnership, pregnancy and maternity, race, religion or belief, sex and sexual orientation'.[8] It is not discrimination on these grounds that most staff members worried about so much as the university's ability to come up with informed and fair assessments of their research.

The Code gives little away about the nuts and bolts of staff selection procedures. 'Responsibility for developing the submission to REF and advising on key decisions' lies with REFSG, whose mandate is to 'develop detailed criteria that reflect the quality level expected by the University within each unit of assessment to be submitted'. It is the job of the REF Steering Group to 'define which units of assessment are to be submitted', 'define the overall quality level to be expected from submissions' and 'notify Heads of Department and relevant staff in writing about decisions made with regard to exclusion or inclusion'. While

---

[4] *Codes of Practice on the selection of staff*, 5. Emphasis added.

[5] *REF 2014: Assessment framework*, para 203.

[6] Lancaster University, *REF 2014 Code of Practice*, 1. http://www.lancaster.ac.uk/depts/research/lancaster/REF2014.html (accessed 20 January 2014).

[7] Lancaster University, *REF 2014: Code of Practice*, 1–2. Emphasis added.

[8] Lancaster University, *REF 2014: Code of Practice*, 1.

there will be 'a uniform process across the University for selecting staff for the REF', we are told, 'the criteria to be used will inevitably vary from discipline to discipline'. REFSG also has the 'responsibility for ensuring that the Code of Practice is consistently implemented'.[9] An appendix sets out the composition of REFSG, together with its terms of reference and a list of the bodies to which it reports. Steering Lancaster's REF are the Pro VC for Research, Associate Deans (Research) for each of the four Faculties, the Head of the Research Support Office and six 'members ad hoc with senior involvement in previous Assessment exercises or on REF panels'. I am sure staff members were all reassured to learn that the HR Manager for Wellbeing, Equality and Diversity would also be 'in attendance'.[10] So what actually happened?

On 16 October 2013 *Nature* ran an article on the REF prominently featuring Lancaster University. 'Two years ago', it began,

> academics at Lancaster … found themselves in the uncomfortable position of being graded. They each had to submit the four best pieces of research that they had published in the previous few years, and then wait for months as small panels of colleagues – each containing at least one person from outside the university – judged the quality of the work.

'The idea of the drill', said Trevor McMillan, Pro VC for Research, was 'to iden-tify areas where we could help people develop their profiles'. Professor McMillan had gone on record earlier in the year in *Times Higher Education*, saying that the removal of QR funding for 2* research meant that higher selectivity for the 2014 REF was 'inevitable'.[11] Help for those who 'failed their evaluations' included 'men-toring from a more experienced colleague, an early start on an upcoming sab-batical or a temporary break from teaching duties'.[12] It would be churlish to deny that some of these things, including provision of teaching release to help people complete books, did occur, benefiting both individuals and the institution – though in two cases known to me, colleagues in History were given support to finish work only to be eventually excluded from the REF. But however supportive its original purpose might have been, Lancaster's Mock REF (or Internal REF, as it was soon rebranded in good Orwellian fashion) soon morphed into the primary mechanism through which staff members were selected for the real thing.

---

[9] Lancaster University, *REF 2014: Code of Practice*, 2.

[10] Lancaster University, *REF 2014: Code of Practice*, 6–7.

[11] Quoted in Paul Jump, 'REF survey eases fears of selective game-playing'. *Times Higher Education*, 17 January 2013.

[12] Professor McMillan is quoted from 'The Greater Good'. *Nature* (editorial), 30 December 2013.

How this selection worked – beyond REFSG and the VC taking the final decisions – is a more difficult question to answer than might be supposed. The details that are absent from the bland generalities of the Code of Practice are walled behind by a Kafkan fortress of confidentiality, which means you risk losing your job by exposing them because breach of confidence is a dismissible offence under Lancaster's disciplinary procedures. But the devil, as always, *is* in the details. The Code of Practice does not even mention the 'small panels of colleagues' that *Nature* claims 'judged the quality of the work'. I have no independent way of knowing whether such panels appraised outputs in Professor McMillan's own Faculty of Science and Technology, but I presume he was not misquoted. The only equivalent known to me in the Faculty of Arts and Social Sciences (FASS) was the regular 'phase' meetings (as they were called) that took place from the summer of 2011 onwards. The people involved in these meetings oversaw the development of the faculty's submission to REF 2014, but so far as I am aware they did not actually read and evaluate research outputs. The phase meetings are not mentioned in the Code of Conduct either, but from what I can infer,[13] they involved departmental Research Directors, Heads of Department, the FASS Associate Dean (Research), the FASS Dean, external assessors and others. One element of their remit was ensuring that all eligible staff would have the necessary four outputs in print by HEFCE's publication deadline of 31 December 2013. But their more important function, in the context of the present discussion, was managing and monitoring the evaluation of outputs.

In the case of History, all eligible staff members were asked to identify four outputs for possible submission to the REF together with one or more reserves. These outputs were all then read by a 'critical friend' – an eminent historian from another UK university – who was *not* a specialist in most of their fields or periods of research. I mean no disrespect in emphasizing this. History is an enormously diverse discipline, in terms of chronology (at Lancaster we have historians of all periods from classical antiquity to the 20th century), geography (we have historians of Britain, several parts of Europe, the Middle East, India, South-east Asia, the Caribbean and the United States), subject matter (economic, political, social, cultural, etc.) and – as with most other humanities and social science disciplines – theoretical standpoints and methodological approaches. To expect *any* one historian, no matter how accomplished he or

---

[13] Principally from the Head of Department's response to my appeal.

she is in his or her field, to be able to judge the quality of research across all these areas of the discipline is absurd. Nonetheless if the critical friend gave staff members a passing grade, the university included them in the REF submission without further review. In other words: *most of what the university regards as 3* or 4* research in the History submission has been certified as such by a single external reviewer, who is not an expert in many of the areas concerned.* If (as the Code of Practice claims) there is a 'uniform process across the University', I would expect the same to be true for other disciplines too.

In all other cases one or more outputs would be subjected to further review. In the Head of Department's words,

> The process ... allowed for (a) internal review alongside the evaluations of the critical friend, in cases where [the friend] had expressed the desirability for this, and (b) external review by independent specialists in other circumstances; for example, when a staff member's profile fell on a borderline, or when the critical friend ... recommended further specialist reading.

It is beyond my comprehension how those involved in the phase meetings were supposed to recognize what a borderline profile was when – according to the same letter – 'the overall aggregate score needed to qualify for inclusion could not be communicated to staff because it was *not known* until the VC met with the REFSG on 24th September 2013'.[14] So far as I am aware the GPA Lancaster required for inclusion in its REF submission – which turned out to be 2.75 in the case of History[15] – has still not been officially published. I don't know which is the more disturbing possibility here: that the GPA cut-off had been decided and guided decisions taken to send outputs out for review long before it was formally adopted by REFSG, which would plainly violate HEFCE's expectations of transparency, or that those involved in the phase meetings were groping around in the dark without any clear guidelines from REFSG, re-reviewing materials and people that for one reason or another they felt were 'risky' whatever scores the critical friend had initially given them.

The group responsible for choosing external reviewers – Head of Department and History Research Director, together with FASS Dean and Associate Dean (Research) – was unrepresentative of the department's research and therefore arguably ill-qualified to choose appropriate reviewers for many staff members' work. It did not contain a single modern historian, even though modernists

---

[14] From the Head of Department's response to my appeal. Emphasis added.

[15] I don't know whether the same cut-off was applied across all UOAs.

constitute a majority in the department.[16] Nor did it include any historian whose work was defined by an interdisciplinary orientation – an important consideration, given the cross-disciplinary background and interests of several department members. It did not consult with those whose research was being assessed over appropriate reviewers, even when that work lay far outside its collective expertise. Further, while reviewers' identities were kept strictly confidential, they seem – even when drawn from other departments within Lancaster University – often to have known the identities of authors. Scores and comments on outputs, by contrast, were communicated to staff – if at all – only in the context of appeals, by which time it was too late to act on them.[17] In many cases it was thought sufficient to approach only *one* reviewer, whose score seems invariably to have replaced that of the critical friend. Options of averaging the scores or going to a third reviewer in cases of serious discrepancy seem not to have been considered.[18] This begs the obvious question: if further review delivered what were regarded as unfailingly more reliable judgements in these cases, why was it not used for all outputs?

One incident graphically reveals both the amateurism of this process and its openness to potential abuse. A (heavily redacted) response to a Freedom of Information Act request from one colleague, whom I shall refer to here as Dr K, uncovered evidence of the History Research Director and an external reviewer meeting to discuss an output *before that reviewer had produced his or her appraisal*. The reviewer (who appears to have been from another department within the university) emailed the research director saying, 'I just need to give you an impression about the REF item you asked me to read' and offered to 'pop into your office' later that day to discuss it. The Research Director responded, 'Will it be helpful? If so, yes'. The reviewer emailed the Research Director a one-paragraph report two days later, asking, 'Will this do?' The

---

[16] 'Decisions were made in consultation between the HoD and Research Director, and the Dean and Associate Dean for Research' – a medieval historian, an early modern historian, a philosopher of religion and a linguist. The 'critical friend' was also not a modern historian. The History Department had 24 full-time academic staff members eligible for submission to the REF at the census date, of whom 15 worked mainly or entirely on modern history.

[17] This occurred in September and October 2013, shortly before the REF submission deadline. In the case of papers read in draft form, early communication of comments might have allowed for revisions before publication. In some universities, timely communication of referees' comments enabled challenges to exclusion from the REF on the grounds of the inadequacy of the reviews. See below, p. 76.

[18] Contrast Canada's SSHRC panel procedures, discussed above (p. 41, note 86).

report ended, 'As a piece of research, this is without doubt fiercely intelligent and stimulating, if rather demanding and non-conformist. But as a potential REF output, it is very risky, in its current form at least'. What is worrying here is that the reviewer appears to be assessing less the *quality* of the piece than its *risk* for the History submission, which is quite a different issue – but one that would be uppermost in the mind of any research director. That such a conversation took place at all undermines any claim that this is a process of genuinely independent review. The reviewer's complaint that the article was difficult, '*at least for someone who is not fully conversant with the exact topic*', also reinforces my doubts as to the specialist qualifications of the reviewers used by the History Department.[19]

This evaluation then triggered a process of re-reviewing other papers that eventuated in Dr K's exclusion from the REF. This is doubly ironic, because not only had Dr K's outputs initially been ranked by the critical friend at 3*/4*, 3* and 2*/3*, well above the 2.75 cut-off, but Human Resources had agreed that Dr K would only need to submit *three* outputs because of special circumstances as defined in HEFCE's Assessment framework. It is mathematically impossible to receive a GPA of 2.75 on three pieces of work marked in integer steps. This means that somebody with four outputs could achieve a GPA of 2.75 while 'carrying' one 2* output (e.g. 3, 3, 3, 2), while somebody with three outputs would have to score 3* across the board to qualify (since 3, 3, 2 yields a GPA of 2.66). To operate a uniform 2.75 cut-off sets the quality bar higher for those with only three outputs, discriminating against precisely those whom the 'special circumstances' rule is intended to help. When Dr K pointed out this anomaly and enquired what the GPA cut-off was for a three-output submission, the question was not answered. The Research Support Office Manager instead blandly asserted, 'we have considered all borderline cases carefully and not simply applied a pre-determined threshold. I am therefore pleased to confirm that we are happy that no-one with a reduction in outputs on the basis of individual special circumstances has been disadvantaged'.[20] This is something that is impossible to verify: we are forced to take the university's word for it. It may or may not be germane that Dr K's work – like that of two other colleagues whose cases I shall discuss later – is interdisciplinary and engages with contemporary cultural theory.

---

[19] Quotations from email correspondence on 14 and 15 March 2012 between History Research Director and an anonymous reviewer for Dr K's proposed REF outputs, supplied to Dr K in response to a Freedom of Information Act request. Emphasis added.

[20] Email from Yvonne Fox to Dr K, 28 October 2013.

Questionable as this process may have been, if the result of further review-ing of outputs was that a staff member's GPA dropped below the requisite threshold, he or she was informed in writing that their research outputs 'were not of the "high quality" … that Lancaster University requires for inclusion' in the REF.[21] There was a right of appeal for individuals who felt they had been unfairly treated in terms of the application of the university's procedures or were victims of discrimination. But there was *no provision for any further reading of outputs* in cases where a staff member disputed the assessments on the basis of which they had been excluded – as seems to have happened in some other universities, even if they were not prepared to admit it publicly.[22] Lancaster's Code of Practice categorically states that

> The decision on the inclusion of staff to the REF is a strategic and qualitative pro-cess in which judgements are made about the quality of research of individual members of staff. *The judgements are subjective*, based on factual information. Hence, disagreement with the decision alone would not be appropriate grounds for an appeal.[23]

This is the ultimate Kafkan twist. The subjectivity of the evaluation is admit-ted, but only as a reason for denying any right of appeal against it.

There is an important contrast to be drawn here with the appeal procedures in the University of Oregon tenure process discussed in Chapter 1. Oregon, too, only allowed appeals on grounds of 'improper procedure … illegal discrimina-tion, or … arbitrariness and capriciousness', but that is where any resemblance stops. Among the procedural grounds for appeal permitted at Oregon were: 'if you feel the departmental report and outside letters have been inadequately summarized for you, or that your case has been misrepresented'.[24] In Lancaster's case, so much of the process is shrouded in secrecy that it would be impossible for individuals involved to know whether their case had been adequately rep-resented or not. Oregon also provided an extremely detailed description of the successive stages through which a tenure or promotion application would pass,

---

[21] Letter quoted in Paolo Palladino, 'Why the REF is bad for the very idea of a university', UCU REFWatch website, 10 December 2013, http://ref.web.ucu.org.uk/2013/12/10/why-the-ref-is-bad-for-the-very-idea-of-the-university/ (accessed 27 January 2014).

[22] A Warwick UCU survey of staff members excluded from the REF, discussed below (pp. 75–7), found a small number of cases where individuals challenged their exclusion on academic grounds and were reinstated, despite the university's official policy.

[23] Lancaster University, *REF 2014 Code of Practice*, 5.

[24] See above, p. 16

detailing the membership of each committee and the role played by each university official in the process, from Head of Department to Provost. In Lancaster, by contrast, staff members are not told where, when, by whom or on what basis recommendations on their inclusion or exclusion in the REF are made (beyond knowing that the ultimate decision lies with REFSG and the VC). *How can one appeal on grounds that 'it is felt that procedure has not been followed'[25] if the procedure in question has never been made public in the first place?*

One of the respects in which HEFCE found draft codes of practice submitted for approval by universities in 2012 most wanting was their provisions for appeal. The Equality and Diversity Panel was especially concerned about 'processes that lacked sufficient independence, so that staff involved in selection decisions were also involved in hearing appeals, or where there was no assurance that appeal outcomes could be implemented before the submission deadline'.[26] The *Assessment framework* reiterates that 'The individuals that handle appeals should be *independent of the decisions about selecting staff*' and that sufficient time must be given for 'members of staff to appeal after they have received … feedback, and for that appeal to be considered by the HEI *before the final selection is made*'.[27] Though HEFCE seems not to have picked it up (but how could they, since so much of what actually went on at faculty and department level did not find its way into the Code of Practice?), Lancaster's final version of the appeal process failed on both counts. The Code sets out a two-level procedure:

> If a member of staff believes that they have appropriate grounds for a complaint they should initially discuss this with their Head of Department, following a request in writing laying out the nature of the concerns. A meeting should take place within 10 days of the request and the outcome followed up within 7 days of the meeting. The Head of Department may consult with the Associate Dean for Research in their faculty as part of their consideration of the appeal.

> Any staff member remaining dissatisfied, should submit formal written notification to the Director of Human Resources within 5 working days of receiving the decision of the original panel, requesting their case be reviewed by a Dean of another faculty.[28]

Not only were the Head of Department and Associate Dean (Research) part of the group that chose external reviewers for outputs and continuously

---

25 Lancaster University, *REF 2014 Code of Practice*, 5.

26 *Codes of Practice on the selection of staff*, 5.

27 *REF 2014: Assessment framework*, para 227.

28 Lancaster University, *REF 2014 Code of Practice*, 5.

involved in the phase meetings that produced the staff profiles upon which REFSG based its final selection decisions, but the Associate Dean (Research) *was also himself a member of REFSG* – the sole body, according to Lancaster's Code of Practice, responsible for selecting staff for REF 2014! Whether the second level of appeal, to the Dean of another faculty, satisfies HEFCE's guidelines is more debatable insofar as Deans did not sit on REFSC.[29] But since the main permitted grounds of appeal were procedural and all Deans were implementing the same supposedly 'uniform process' within their own faculties, they are not the most obviously independent parties the university might have chosen for such a task.

As regards timeliness, History staff members were formally notified of REFSG's selection decisions in late September/early October 2013. The Head of Department had verbally warned some colleagues of the likelihood of their exclusion earlier in the summer; others at that point were still having outputs read. The deadline for appeals to be submitted was 8 October. This left, in some instances, *less than a week* to prepare an appeal. The time given for launching the second level of appeal was a mere *five days*. In neither case would this provide appellants with enough time to obtain any information relevant to their appeal from the university under the Freedom of Information Act (as they had a legal right to do).[30] Faculty Deans were still hearing second-stage appeals at the end of October. The deadline for the university to upload its REF submission to the HEFCE website was 29 November 2013. As anyone involved will testify, the logistics of coordinating the submission across the university were difficult enough without having to accommodate any last-minute changes. It is hard to see how this timetable could have realistically allowed for reinstatement of any excluded individuals.

It would have been especially difficult for the university if reinstatement would have a knock-on effect for the impact element of the REF submission. Under HEFCE's rules, the number of impact case studies each UOA had to submit was a function of the number of staff members returned.[31] If a UOA contained 24 staff, for instance, only three impact case studies would be required, each of which would then account for 5.33% of the overall assessment. Adding another staff member would both require a fourth case study and reduce the contribution of each existing case study to 4%.[32] These studies are extremely detailed, laboriously researched documents; they cannot be produced at the

---

[29] They are, however, members of the University Management Advisory Group (UMAG), to which REFSG reports.

[30] Institutions are allowed 20 working days to comply with FOI requests.

[31] See *REF 2014: Assessment framework*, para 156.

[32] Impact counts for 20% of the overall assessment, of which case studies count for 80% irrespective of their number. The other 20% is for the general impact narrative.

drop of a hat. They also count for a significantly greater proportion of the aggregate REF score than any one individual's outputs (which for a 24-member UOA would be 2.5%). The damage done by a weak impact study, the reasoning goes, will far outweigh the benefits the addition of any marginal individual can bring to a UOA. It is now widely alleged – if difficult to prove – that (in the words of Times Higher Education's Paul Jump) 'Some institutions ... determined the number of academics they submitted according to the number of high-quality case studies they could muster. Indeed, at least one institution – the University of Leicester – admits that it envisaged doing so'.[33]

I do not know whether this was a factor in Lancaster's decisions regarding the History submission, nor whether verdicts on appeals could have altered the number of impact case studies required. It may or may not be significant, however, that had all eligible full-time History staff employed at Lancaster on the census date been entered in REF 2014, the headcount would have been exactly 24.0 FTE. If nobody from the department's full-time academic staff was excluded from the REF submission, in other words, there would have been no room to include anyone in the UOA from outside the department (as happened in RAE 2008) or who was on a post-retirement or other fractional contract (as were two highly productive History professors in 2014)[34] without the UOA needing to produce another impact case study.

Against this background it would be interesting to know how many appeals were launched at Lancaster University and what proportion of these (if any) succeeded. All three appeals that I know of in the History Department[35] were rejected. My own was one of them. The substance of its arguments – that the procedures through which I was selected for inclusion in the REF violated the guidelines set out in HEFCE's Assessment framework and discriminated against colleagues who were excluded – is set out in the next section of this chapter. I am not allowed to say why the appeal was turned down. The report of the Dean who heard the second stage of appeal was marked 'Confidential'. When

---

[33] Jump, 'The REF: how was it for you?'

[34] These count as Category A staff for REF purposes. See REF 2014: Assessment framework, para 78 and especially 79(c).

[35] Professor Palladino, whose case I discuss later, refused to appeal on principle. There may have been other appeals, but the university does not make such numbers public. I would not expect a huge number of appeals because the permitted grounds for appeal have been drawn so narrowly. Times Higher Education used information received under FOI Act requests from 145 universities to show that in RAE 2008, 190 academics appealed against exclusion, and 58 (30.5%) of these appeals were upheld. This compares with 52,401 staff submitted. Zoe Corbyn, 'Almost 200 academic staff fight against RAE exclusion'. Times Higher Education, 7 August 2008.

I wrote Human Resources enquiring whether I might nonetheless make its contents public on my blog (since, I said, 'I have always been in favour of presenting all sides of an argument'),[36] the Director's answer was that it 'must not be reported in full (with or without names), nor summarized or paraphrased in any way ... in your blog or any other means of communication outside the University' – which, of course, includes this book.[37] I was permitted to report only the fact that the appeal had been rejected.

3.2 TRANSPARENCY, CONSISTENCY, ACCOUNTABILITY AND INCLUSIVITY

'The four main underlying principles' the funding councils expected to govern selection of staff for REF 2014 were 'transparency, consistency, accountability, and inclusivity'.[38] HEFCE unambiguously spelled out what it meant by these in its *Assessment framework and guidance on submissions*; so there was no excuse for universities not to know exactly what was required of them. We know that Lancaster University's Code of Conduct was approved by HEFCE, but we have also seen that this code provides little or no detail about what went on at faculty and department level. The question I now want to ask is: to what extent were the *practices* at Lancaster consistent with these principles?

The university certainly made its Code of Practice 'available in an easily accessible format', 'publicised [it] to all academic staff ... including on the staff intranet', ensured that copies were mailed to absent staff and had a 'programme of communication activity to disseminate the code of practice', which was 'documented in the code'. Whether, on the other hand, the Code of Practice or program of communication could be said to '*explain* the processes related to selection of staff for submission', as HEFCE also requires, is another matter.[39] Faculty- and department-level processes related to selection of staff were *not* covered in the Code of Practice, and nor in my view were they adequately communicated to staff in any other forum.

History staff members were informed that the critical friend would read all their outputs and that this evaluation would somehow feed into final

---

[36] Email from author to Helen Ratcliffe, Lancaster University HR, 28 October 2013.

[37] Email from Andy Clarke, Director of HR at Lancaster University, 1 November 2013. For more details, see my blog posts 'Lancaster REF appeal: Castle closed, reasons confidential' (28 October 2013) and 'GAG' (posted 1 November 2013).

[38] *Codes of Practice on the selection of staff*, 3.

[39] *REF 2014: Assessment framework*, para 204. Emphasis added. Compare Lancaster University, *REF 2014 Code of Practice*, 5.

decisions on selection for the REF. They also knew that their work might be sent out for further review. But they were *not* told: the scores the critical friend had given their outputs or the criteria employed in assigning them; the circumstances that would trigger a further review of one or more outputs; the basis on which further readers were chosen and who was responsible for selecting them; or the GPA needed to qualify for submission to the 2014 REF. By criteria employed in assigning scores I mean, specifically, *how* the university's evaluators distinguished 'world-leading' (4*) from 'internationally excellent' (3*) and 'internationally recognized' (2*) research. Nowadays, UK universities routinely require their academic staff to operationalize such descriptors in everything from promotion guidelines to undergraduate handbooks; students want to know exactly what they have to do in an essay to get an A grade. As we saw in Chapter 2, even REF panels carried out 'calibration exercises' at the start of their deliberations to ensure 'consistency in … standards of assessment'. I fail to see why Lancaster cannot spell out the indicators used to determine degrees of excellence when it comes to grading its own staff for the REF. We are not in Bahram Bekhradnia's ideal world in which 'people wake up and find they got a score but don't know how they got it'. Or maybe, on second thoughts, we are.

When, in October 2013, I asked my Head of Department where information on these matters might be found, I was told: 'As far as I'm aware, the evaluative procedures for arriving at decisions have not been published on the website, and in any case they will differ from Faculty to Faculty and department to department'.[40] It is precisely because of such differences, of course, that one would expect these procedures to be published *in addition* to the Code of Practice if HEFCE's transparency requirements were to be met. The Head later claimed that 'The process to be followed in History was explained to staff in Department Meetings'[41] from 2011 through 2013, but in my opinion this is not borne out by the written record. Though there are reports from the departmental Research Director at virtually every meeting, the minutes are silent on the points I have listed, and no written description of these procedures was published at either faculty or department level. HEFCE in any case required Codes of Conduct – which it expected to adequately describe the evaluative procedures to which staff members would be subject – to be publicized on staff websites and communicated to staff who were absent from work (e.g. on sick leave or sabbatical). Briefing in department meetings satisfies neither requirement. So much, then, for transparency.

---

[40] Email from the Head of Department to author, 3 October 2013.

[41] From the Head of Department's response to my appeal.

The university's disregard of HEFCE's guidelines with regard to accountability was, if anything, even more blatant. The *Assessment framework* requires that 'Responsibilities should be clearly defined, and *individuals and bodies that are involved in selecting staff for REF submissions* should be *identified by name or role*'. It also stipulates that 'Operating criteria and terms of reference for *individuals, committees, advisory groups and any other bodies concerned with staff selection* should be made readily available to all individuals and groups concerned'.[42] The university maintains that because 'the "phase" meetings between RDs, HoDs, Deans and ADRs held within FASS at regular intervals following the mock REF had a reporting capacity',[43] they did not qualify as 'individuals and bodies … concerned with staff selection' as understood by HEFCE. From a common sense point of view, this distinction is fatuous, but in this instance, I think even the lawyers would have trouble defending the university's casuistry. The *Assessment framework* is explicit and unambiguous. It requires that 'Where a committee or committees have *designated REF responsibilities – whether it is at departmental, faculty, UOA or central level –* these should be *detailed in the code of practice*, including, for each committee':

- how the committee has been formed;
- its membership;
- the definition of its position within *the advisory or decision-making process*
- […].

The following details should be provided about its mode of operation:

- the criteria that it will use in carrying out its functions;
- the method by which these criteria are communicated … .[44]

The university might, I suppose, be tempted to employ the wholly circular (and totally Kafkan) argument that the fact that the bodies and individuals in question are not designated in the Code of Practice means they do not fall under this rule. But the passages I have italicized put it beyond dispute that the rule applies to *all* committees, panels, groups or individuals involved in the REF, whether their role was decision-making or advisory, and whether their activities took place at departmental, faculty or university level. We might again contrast the identification of committee members involved at every level in the North American tenure and promotion procedures discussed in Chapter 1.

---

[42] *REF 2014: Assessment framework*, para 204.

[43] From the Head of Department's response to my appeal.

[44] *REF 2014: Assessment framework*, paras 209 and 210. Emphasis added.

HEFCE's third 'underlying principle' is consistency. 'It is essential', says the *Assessment framework*, 'that policy in respect of staff selection is *consistent across the institution* and that the code of practice is *implemented uniformly*'.[45] I suspect that in practice there will have been considerable variation in evaluation procedures between Lancaster's departments and faculties, in part precisely because this level of the selection process was not formalized in the Code of Conduct. I am still puzzled by Professor McMillan's 'small panels' and would be interested to know how widespread their use was and how they were composed; at least they hold out the possibility of multiple assessments of outputs being built into the process from the start rather than everything hinging on the judgement of one critical friend. Even within FASS, rumour has it that some departments developed procedures that resulted in much more inclusive outcomes than in the History Department – consulting individuals over who might be suitable external reviewers for their work, for example, or discarding obviously aberrant scores. I have no quarrel with such variations insofar as they reflect different disciplinary expectations. But Lancaster's secrecy over the membership, terms of reference and operating criteria of *any* bodies involved in the REF staff selection process below REFSG level makes it impossible to ascertain whether colleagues were treated consistently across the university or not.

There was manifest inconsistency in the treatment of colleagues *within* History, insofar as some were selected for the REF on the basis of the critical friend's judgement alone, while others had their work subjected to further review. Given that the friend was not an expert in many of the research fields at issue, while further reviewers were intended to be field specialists,[46] it could be argued that the bar was being set higher for some than for others – that those whose work was sent for further review had to impress readers who actually knew something about their area and could do more than appreciate the coherence of the argument, admire the prose style and count the footnotes. But the more important point here is that whether or not somebody's work was sent out for specialist review depended not on its intrinsic merits (however measured) but on *whether the critical friend felt confident to assess it*. This installed a wholly arbitrary jeopardy right at the heart of the evaluative process. As I suggested earlier in connection with Dr K's case, this may have worked to the particular disadvantage of those scholars in the department whose interdisciplinary approaches to history were grounded in contemporary social and cultural theory.

---

[45]   *REF 2014: Assessment framework*, para 204.

[46]   I am not sure they always were, for reasons set out above (the composition of the group that chose reviewers and their unwillingness to consult with authors on fields from which they might be drawn).

One such colleague was Paolo Palladino, who – perhaps not incidentally – carries the title of Professor of History and Theory. Informed in late September 2013 that his four outputs 'were not of the "high quality" ... that Lancaster University requires for inclusion' in its REF submission, Professor Palladino (in his own words):

> refused to partake in the officially sanctioned mechanisms of appeal and ... opted instead to challenge the culture of silence and secrecy surrounding exclusion by writing an open letter to the Dean of the Faculty of Arts and Social Sciences and the Vice-Chancellor of Lancaster University.[47]

The issue, he argued in this letter, was *not* one of quality. The crux of the problem was rather that:

> the internal preparations for REF reward disciplinary orthodoxy by resting, for reasons of economy, upon the evaluations of a single reader per Unit of Assessment (UoA) and by expecting that each member of staff returned should fit within the narrative of one of the UoA submissions. Consequently, it is not possible to accommodate a researcher whose output is 'recognised internationally in terms of originality, significance and rigour', but whose work cuts across the domains of a number of UoAs and thus must in all likelihood fall short of the most common assumptions about what constitute the 'highest standards of excellence' (grade 4) for each and every UoA involved.[48]

At the time of writing, this letter has yet to receive a reply from either the FASS Dean or the VC.

Professor Palladino later expanded on these arguments in a longer piece published on the UCU's *REFWatch* website. The squeezing out of interdisciplinary work, he suggests, is the 'inevitable consequence of the drive to reduce the mounting costs of national research assessment exercises and our collective refusal to countenance the adoption of metrics, all of which has resulted in the devolution of responsibility for the containment of these costs onto the universities'. It is not so much that there is a conspiracy against interdisciplinary work either nationally or locally (even if 'many of our colleagues are less than sanguine about the importance of interdisciplinary research and its urge to call into question disciplinary orthodoxies'). The pressures are structural. So long as REF panels:

---

[47] Palladino, 'Why the REF is bad for the very idea of a university'.

[48] I reproduced this on my blog: see 'Kafkarna continues: REF gloves off at Lancaster University' (posted 28 September 2013).

are organized along disciplinary lines and far more tightly than ever was the case under the RAE ... all institutions interested in maximizing their returns cannot but seek to exclude any research output that might be regarded as not fitting securely within the confines of disciplinary narratives and their orthodoxies. [49]

Once again fears of risk trump considerations of quality.

Interdisciplinary research has long been recognized as a problem for the British research assessment system, with a variety of remedies being tried from RAE to RAE, and none of them proving very satisfactory. The Roberts report expressed concern over 'the disciplinary basis of the RAE and its effects upon interdisciplinarity and multidisciplinarity'[50] with regard to RAE 2001. A *Times Higher Education* leader voiced the same fears in the run-up to RAE 2008, commenting that although the

> guidelines for the ... RAE say it will encourage interdisciplinary research by allowing its specialist panels to cross-refer material to each other ... many academics still doubt such work will be taken as seriously as research that advances a specific field of study. So the cautious move is to omit academics whose work takes an interdisciplinary approach.[51]

Plus ça change, we might think; the eternal return of the ever same. Only in REF 2014, not only was the number of disciplinary panels almost halved (and external specialist reviewers who might have looked at interdisciplinary outputs dispensed with altogether), but panels were also instructed to use cross-referencing only 'exceptionally'.[52]

Professor Palladino's outputs bounced back and forth like hot potatoes between History and Sociology UOAs, neither of which was in the end prepared to assume the risk of having research that transcended – or should I say, transgressed – its disciplinary boundaries assessed by a subpanel constituted on the basis of a single discipline. I do not know how the individual outputs were scored, but that is beside the point here. Two things make this case especially poignant. The first is that as Head of Department in 2007–2009, Professor Palladino played a major part in conceiving and implementing an extensive series of reforms to practices in teaching, administration and research support

---

[49] Palladino, 'Why the REF is bad for the very idea of a university'.

[50] *Review of research assessment: Report by Sir Gareth Roberts*, 5.

[51] 'Leader: Excluding the many for the sake of the few'. *Times Higher Education*, 2 February 2007.

[52] *REF 2014: Panel Criteria*, para 111.

aimed at improving the History Department's disappointing performance in the 2008 RAE. He did so in the teeth of considerable opposition from within the department. The second is that he was promoted to a personal chair in 2011 *on the basis of the same portfolio of publications* as were deemed two years later to be inadequate for the REF. For professorial promotions at Lancaster, the university solicits the views of a minimum of *six external referees* whom it requires to be:

> eminent and independent and chosen with care: their departments should be of at least comparable standing with that of the candidate; they must be able to comment on the national or international reputation of the candidate; they will be normally be of Professorial (or equivalent) level and enjoy national or international standing *within the candidate's subject area*. The expectation is that normally all referees will be of international standing and able to comment on the international reputation of the candidate and that normally two will work outside the UK.

The university stresses that such referees 'can be especially useful in assessing the contribution of the candidate to and their standing (national and international) in *scholarship and research*'.[53] But apparently in this case, the critical friend and whatever other ad hoc assessors the university employed delivered more credible verdicts.

Another History department member – whose work also draws on contemporary cultural theory – had a GPA of 2.75 after the initial reading and evaluation of outputs by the critical friend. That should have been the end of the matter, since 2.75 was the qualifying GPA for inclusion. But Dr M, as I shall call this colleague, was nonetheless left out of History's REF submission. For reasons that are unclear to me, one of the articles the friend had originally scored at 3* was sent to an external reader who graded it as 2*, thereby reducing Dr M's GPA to 2.5. Those responsible went with the lower score and refused to commission a further review. What is most troubling here – at least to any believer in peer review – is that the article in question was published in *Past and Present*, which is regarded by most UK historians as one of the top historical journals, if not *the* leading historical journal in the English language. Dr M had also been urged by the editor of a major specialist journal in the field to withdraw the article from consideration at *Past and Present* (who had not at that point finally accepted it) with the promise that it would be published as a lead article in this second journal as the centrepiece of a themed issue. Once again the subjective

---

53 Lancaster University, 'Promotion to Readership and Personal Chair: Procedures and Criteria'. http://www.lancaster.ac.uk/hr/total-reward/files/ccrcrit.html (accessed 3 January 2014).

judgements of university-appointed assessors trumped the peer evaluations of leading professional journals in the field.[54]

This 'tale of the general crappiness of UKHE and its management' caught the eye of Guy Halsall, Professor of Medieval History at the University of York, and author of the widely read blog *Historian on the Edge*. 'One thing', he reflected, 'stands out for me. That is the decision of a couple of people within the dept and one "critical friend" to grade a piece accepted by *Past and Present* at "2" (basically, for those unfamiliar with the labyrinth, a low score)'. He continues:

> As we all know, good journals publish (what we consider to be) bad articles, (what we consider to be) bad books get published in good book series, for all sorts of reasons – usually for simply saying what the great and good think ought to be said in the right sort of way, but sometimes for more nefarious reasons. Be that as it may, though, *Past and Present* has one of the most rigorous refereeing systems in existence. An article has to go through the hands of a lot of smart people before it is accepted and appears … The grading of such an article at 2 strikes me as an example of monumental egotism – that this person's view is **so** much better than that of the six leading scholars who read it and accepted it for publication in the country's leading academic historical journal. That level of egotism and arrogance disgusts me. It is sadly not atypical of the profession, though.[55]

This is an appropriate point to recall that HEFCE's fourth 'underlying principle' governing staff selection for the REF was supposed to have been *inclusivity*. It is a principle that seems to have been interpreted extraordinarily narrowly at Lancaster and elsewhere. For understandable reasons, HEFCE's documents pay a lot of attention to the requirements of the UK's 2010 Equalities Act and related legislation. Nobody wanted lawsuits. But it is too easily forgotten that the provisions set out in the *Assessment framework* on discrimination, special circumstances and mandatory equality impact assessments are all means to a greater end, which is 'to develop working methods and assessment criteria that encourage HEIs to submit the work of *all of their excellent researchers,* including those whose ability to produce four outputs or work productively throughout the assessment period had been constrained for reasons covered by equality legislation'.[56] A separate paragraph reiterates: 'The code should promote an inclusive environment, enabling institutions to identify *all eligible staff who have*

---

[54] I reported this case in my blog on 5 October 2013 under the title 'Update from Wonderland: the Lancaster History REF farce goes on'.

[55] Guy Halsall, 'Lancaster latest'. 15 October 2013, http://600transformer.blogspot. com/2013_10_01_archive.html (accessed 28 January 2014).

[56] *REF 2014: Assessment framework*, para 201.

produced excellent research for submission to the REF'.[57] As it turned out, sickness, pregnancy and disability were far from the only factors keeping excellent researchers out of the REF (though HEFCE would do well not to ignore mounting evidence of continuing structural discrimination against women, resulting in a smaller proportion being submitted compared with men).[58]

If institutions are to be inclusive in this wider sense, their procedures must be capable of determining whether outputs do or do not constitute 'excellent research' – which requires *competent and honest intellectual evaluation,* not second-guessing of REF panels and speculation on risk. It is here, I believe, that the processes used to select staff for Lancaster's History submission were most obviously flawed from both a moral and an intellectual point of view. They could not be trusted to determine excellence (or its absence), because *they did not meet the international standards of peer review through which the academy normally expects such judgements to be made.* Judged against this yardstick, they were dangerously arbitrary and subjective – especially when individuals' academic reputations and future career prospects were at stake. HEFCE's decision to publish names of staff included in all REF submissions[59] means that it will be relatively easy to identify those who were excluded, to their possible disadvantage in the job market, funding competitions and other academic contexts. Elsewhere in Lancaster, these shortcomings were acknowledged. Writing in 2012, Michael Kosch, Professor of Physics and Associate Dean (Research) for the Faculty of Science and Technology, warned that 'some weaknesses in the mock REF exercise are apparent, for example in many cases there was only one external reviewer per department, no doubt with expert knowledge but not in all the relevant areas'.[60] HEFCE had urged universities to use their mock REFs to iron out problems with their selection process, but this is one lesson that does not seem to have gotten through to the Faculty of Arts and Social Sciences.

---

[57] *REF 2014: Assessment framework,* para 204.

[58] See Graziosi, 'Sex and the REF'.

[59] HEFCE, 'Arrangements for the publication of results: REF 2014' (April 2014), para 15. http://www.ref.ac.uk/pubs/arrangementsforthepublicationofresults/ (accessed 25 June 2014). A HEFCE official signing herself only as Vicky confirmed that 'each submission we publish will include a list of the names of staff that were included in that submission ... We will also be publishing a separate list of all the outputs included in the submission which will include the majority of the metadata that was provided in the submission, such as title, publisher and year of publication' (email to author from info@ref.ac.uk, 26 June 2014).

[60] Michael Kosch, 'In preparation for REF2014 – Mock REF and Units of Assessment'. *SciTech Bulletin* #125 [nd (summer 2012)]. http://www.lancaster.ac.uk/sci-tech/bulletin/0125-2012-05-04.html (accessed 23 January 2014).

3.3 THE NATIONAL PICTURE: HOW WIDESPREAD WERE THE ABUSES?

How typical of British universities was this cavalier approach to selecting staff for the REF? It remains difficult to answer this question. Universities were generally reluctant to spell out their intentions prior to the REF for fear of giving away too much to competitors, while the data that will allow comparison of numbers of staff eligible for submission with numbers submitted at the level of individual universities and UOAs have not yet been made public. The Higher Education Statistics Agency (HESA) has announced plans to publish this information on 18 December 2014. No comparable figures were published for RAE 2008; so it was not possible to ascertain whether universities had inflated their position in league tables by only submitting their 'best' researchers. Assuming the data are not withheld at the last minute (as they were in 2008), the HESA figures should allow league tables to be constructed for REF 2014 that are weighted for numbers of staff submitted, giving a less misleading overall picture than did RAE 2008.[61]

In the meantime the indications are that on the national scale, changes to the QR funding formula did not result in the wholesale exclusions of eligible staff that many had anticipated. Universities submitted the research of 52,077 staff for assessment in REF 2014 compared with 52,401 in the RAE 2008.[62] According to HESA there were 179,040 academics employed in UK institutions of higher education in 2008–2009 compared with 181,385 in 2011–2012.[63] This means 28.7% of academics were entered in REF 2014 compared with 29.3% in RAE 2008 – a fall of less than 1 percentage point (0.6%).[64] However, data released by HEFCE in February 2014 shows an uneven pattern of submission across disciplines. The numbers of staff submitted to Panel B (physical sciences) in the 2014 REF rose by 8% over RAE 2008, while Panels A (life sciences), C (social sciences)

---

[61] See Jump, 'REF "contextual data" decision could enrich league tables'.

[62] HEFCE, 'REF submissions received'.

[63] HESA, 'Staff in UK Higher Education'. http://www.hesa.ac.uk/content/ view/2694/393/ (accessed 29 January 2014). These figures include those on fixed-term and part-time contracts – the new academic 'precariat', whose numbers, in the UK as in the United States, are growing exponentially. Those on full-time (65%) or permanent/open-ended contracts (63.8%) cannot always be assumed to be in positions with a research component. Year 2011 is the latest year for which HESA gives data.

[64] Paul Jump, 'REF selectivity fears "prove unfounded"'. *Times Higher Education*, 5 December 2013.

and D (humanities) saw decreases of 3%, 3% and 5%, respectively.[65] While we cannot be sure of the significance of these figures without knowing the overall numbers of staff employed in these disciplines on the REF census date, they raise the possibility that universities may have been more selective in some disciplines – most notably in the humanities – than others.

I would also interject another note of caution. Though the total number of staff submitted in REF 2014 represents only a small reduction from RAE 2008, it contrasts with a 3.6% *increase* projected in a HEFCE survey of universities' intentions published in January 2013, less than a year before the submission deadline.[66] It was no doubt with relief that Sir Alan Langlands, David Eastwood's successor as chief executive of HEFCE, welcomed this survey as indicating 'that higher education institutions continue to attach importance to identifying all of the excellent research undertaken by their staff, and to having its excellence validated through robust expert review'.[67] An increase in staff numbers submitted is the last thing anyone would have expected at that point in time. One possible explanation is that although total academic staff numbers stayed relatively steady over the period, the proportion of research-active staff may have risen. Alternately, a significant number of staff members may have been performing at a higher level than in 2008. In either case, the level of selectivity required to produce the eventual modest reduction in total numbers as compared with RAE 2008 would be higher than it appears from the overall figures and is perhaps more accurately indicated by the gap between the *projected* and *actual* staff numbers submitted.

Unfortunately, the only way we have to count the number of research-active staff is by their inclusion in universities' submissions to the REF, and the adoption by some universities of a GPA cut-off or other 'strategic' criteria for inclusion has invalidated this as a measure. But the fact is that out of 54,269 academics universities informed HEFCE they were intending to submit in REF 2014, only 52,007 were entered. In other words, 2,262 staff did *not* make the cut rather than the 324 suggested by the crude comparison of submissions to the 2008 RAE and the 2014 REF. By this measure, 4.3% of academics who would likely have counted as 'research-active' in RAE 2008 were not entered in

---

[65] HEFCE, 'More data on submissions to the REF'. 12 February 2014. http://www.hefce. ac.uk/news/newsarchive/2014/news85460.html (accessed 16 February 2014). These are FTE (rather than headcount) figures for category A (full-time) staff, rounded to the nearest 0.5%.

[66] Jump, 'REF survey eases fears of selective game-playing'.

[67] Quoted in Paul Jump, 'Staff submitted to REF likely to go above RAE total'. *Times Higher Education*, 15 January 2013.

REF 2014, not 0.6%.[68] These would have been individuals who were regarded as research active at the time of the HEFCE survey (otherwise universities would not have included them in their projections) but were subsequently excluded from submissions on 'quality' or 'strategic' grounds. If it turns out that these staff were disproportionately concentrated in particular universities, as seems probable, then the benign national picture suggested by the totals may mask much higher exclusion rates within some institutions.

The mere fact – if it is a fact – that a minority of universities may have been more selective in choosing who to enter in the REF than others does not in itself, of course, necessarily mean that there was anything wrong with their selection processes. But there is abundant, if often anecdotal, evidence that Lancaster is not the only institution to have played fast and loose with HEFCE's staff selection guidelines. A UCU survey of staff members excluded from Warwick University's REF 2014 submission attracted 44 responses – the largest in the branch's history. Most complained that the university's 'Selection criteria are not transparent, are applied inconsistently and with little regard to inclusivity – in contravention of the stated REF principles'. Four people, it was claimed, were 'excluded purely on "strategic grounds"', while 'A few staff' were 'excluded simply because their department has insufficient impact statements'. Twenty-six respondents were allegedly excluded because their outputs did not meet a GPA threshold (3.0 was usual, but some departments demanded two 4* papers). As we saw earlier, Warwick was accused by the UCU of being highly selective in RAE 2008. Its management would likely point to the fact that it was the first university founded in the 1960s or later to be admitted to the Russell Group as proof that the policy worked. It is a specious argument: the second 'new' university admitted to the club would be the University of York (which joined the Russell Group in 2012), whose VC Brian Cantor was among the most vocal critics[69] of selectivity game-playing in RAE 2008.

On the evidence of this survey, Warwick's procedures for judging the quality of outputs in REF 2014 seem to have been every bit as questionable as Lancaster's. Some departments, it was alleged, 'disregarded publications not in journals and based their decisions on journal rankings', contrary to HEFCE's own emphatically stated position. Respondents also claimed that 'Research is often excluded on the subjective judgement of Heads of Department without having been independently appraised by experts external to the university, and

[68] This calculation does not take into account any individuals who had already been excluded in universities' projections for the HEFCE survey.

[69] See Brian Cantor, 'How can we measure the quality of research without quantity data?' *Times Higher Education*, 11 December 2008.

in some cases, externals were asked to "confirm" HoDs' assessments, not to read and assess the work independently'. It says little for Warwick's transparency that 19 respondents *did not know* whether internal or external experts reviewed their work, while 28 had no idea how many assessors had read their outputs. Even though there were often 'crucial differences in grades awarded for the same output by different reviewers', the UCU claims, 'The university's approach seems to be that ... if there is a difference of opinion whether an output is "internationally excellent" (3* or 4*) or merely "internationally recognised" (2*) then it should be excluded'. This, too, echoes the Lancaster History Department's rules of thumb. Both universities appear to have regarded differences between reviewers as a sign that an output was 'risky', instead of giving authors the benefit of the doubt or consulting a further reviewer.

The Warwick survey expressed 'concerns with the way assessors have been chosen', with some respondents suggesting: 'in some cases assessors did not have the necessary expertise to give an authoritative opinion'. Only five respondents were allowed to read reviews of their work, while seven were shown edited parts of them. Once again the contrast with North American norms of transparency should not be allowed to pass unremarked. What are British universities so concerned to hide? This *is* Bekhradnia's dystopian world in which people wake up and find they got a score but don't know how they got it. Warwick staff were apparently not given the right 'to correct factual errors and rebut erroneous arguments' in reviewers' reports, though – unlike at Lancaster – 'A small number of [UCU] members have been granted a right of appeal on substantive, academic grounds (despite the university having said that it would only hear appeals within the context of Equality Legislation) and been reinstated'. Carol Rutter, a Professor in the English Department, claims that outputs originally evaluated at 1 x 4* and 3 x 3* were downgraded to 1 x 3* and 3 x 2*, resulting in her exclusion from the REF, but that after she presented 12 letters endorsing her work from international authorities in her field to her Head of Department and the Warwick VC Nigel Thrift she was included in the university's submission. Any admission that assessors' judgements might conceivably be fallible is welcome, but there is an obvious issue of consistency here: if the privilege of appealing on academic grounds was extended to some, why was it not extended to all? Responding to these allegations, a spokesman for Warwick University insisted that '*formal* appeals had been launched on an equality basis only' and 'disputed claims that selection criteria had been applied inconsistently'.[70]

---

[70] Penny Sarchet, 'REF procedures "shambolic" at Warwick', *Research Fortnight*, 13 November 2013. http://pennysarchet.wordpress.com (accessed 12 August 2014). Emphasis added.

There are allegations that Warwick treated interdisciplinary research 'particularly badly'. In no case, needless to say, was an interdisciplinary orientation 'given as the reason for exclusion but sixteen academics [out of 44 respondents] said their work was interdisciplinary'. These scholars reported a variety of ways in which their work had, in their view, been disadvantaged – even according to the REF panels' own limited procedures for handling interdisciplinary research – but the result in each case was the same:

> Some said it had not been reviewed as such in a manner consistent with the way such research will be assessed by the REF Panels, but instead had been done according to narrow disciplinary criteria. Some members reported that the university's REF selection committee had refused to consider requesting cross-referring their research as laid down in the published REF procedure. One member, whose research was published in leading interdisciplinary journals, discovered it had not even been flagged as interdisciplinary by the committee on the REF2 form. It seems particularly worrying for the future of British research if institutions like Warwick have decided that their chances of doing well in the REF league table are optimised by excluding interdisciplinary research, some of which is often among the most innovative, original and important.

Unsurprisingly perhaps, what most concerned respondents to the Warwick survey was

> the consequences of exclusion for their careers. They are unsure if they are in good standing or not … they have been told in writing that their research falls short of 'the university's required standard in terms of quality' but informed only orally that they are still in good standing.[71]

Paolo Palladino experienced exactly the same refusal to provide written confirmation of verbal reassurances he had been given at Lancaster. 'My Head of Department', he writes,

> has been and still is very supportive. I have valued greatly his reassurances that I remain an active and valued contributor to the departmental research portfolio, and that the terms of the letter informing me about my exclusion were 'mistaken' because my exclusion was in fact on 'strategic grounds'.

But he goes on:

> I have asked nonetheless for formal confirmation that I am not failing to meet any of my responsibilities as a member of the Department of History. I have

---

[71] All quotations from Warwick UCU, 'Warwick survey shows REF rules being bypassed and selection guidelines ignored' (November 2013), 1–3, https://www.warwickucu.org.uk/sites/default/files/Warwick%20REF%20survey.pdf

also asked for confirmation that, in future years, the balance of my teaching, research and administration, as reflected in the workload allocation model, will not be outwith departmental norms, and that I will continue to benefit from the mechanisms within the Department of History and the Faculty of Arts and Social Sciences to support the engagement of individual staff in academic research and bids for external funding. No formal acknowledgment or response to the request has yet been received. I have spoken to my Head of Department about this and all that he could do was to smile knowingly about the absurdity of our predicament.[72]

In the period leading up to the REF, a number of universities made very hawkish noises about what would happen to staff members not included in REF submissions. A UCU national survey carried out in June 2013 attracted 7500 respondents. Of these, only 35% agreed that their own institution's staff selection procedures were transparent, and 6% claimed that senior managers selected staff for the REF without any input from peer review. While 53% 'feared losing their jobs if they failed to meet REF criteria', only 4% had actually 'been informed by a manager or senior colleague that failure to meet REF expectations will result in redundancy'. One thing a regime like the REF does very effectively is to create a perpetual climate of anxiety, especially when many of the rules of the game are not known. Confirming the suspicions I voiced earlier about a minority of institutions' behaviour sullying a generally rosier national picture, however, respondents at some universities told a very different story. Threats of redundancy were reported by 29% of respondents at Middlesex University; 24% at the University of Leicester; 21% at City University, London; 18% at Queen's University, Belfast; 13% at the University of Birmingham and 11% at the Universities of Sussex, Cardiff and Warwick.

Universities founded in the 1960s seem to have been prominent among the REF hawks. At Warwick, 17% of respondents claimed they had been told to expect disciplinary procedures for non-submission, compared with 2% of all respondents. At the University of Essex, 29% of respondents reported having been told to expect denial of promotion, 20% to expect transfer to inferior terms and conditions and 59% to expect to be moved to teaching-focused contracts if they failed to meet the criteria for REF selection. Sector averages for these threats were very much lower at 10%, 4% and 12%, respectively. At the University of East Anglia, 36% of respondents had been warned of 'capability procedures to address underperformance' if they were excluded from the REF (which compares with a sector average of 4%).[73] Warwick, Sussex, Essex and

---

[72] Palladino, 'Why the REF is bad for the very idea of a university'.

[73] Paul Jump, 'UCU uncovers high price of failure to hit REF targets'. *Times Higher Education*, 3 October 2013.

East Anglia were all 1960s foundations, as was Lancaster. All these universities were also members of the 1994 Group (as was Leicester), though Warwick left to join the Russell Group in 2008. While I do not think there is any single factor that unites all REF hawks, these universities do share a structural insecurity that comes from being research-intensive without the student numbers or big science infrastructure of most Russell Group schools. They are among the institutions that have most to lose from further concentration of QR funding and may have been feeling especially vulnerable following the collapse of the 1994 Group in 2013.

On 8 August 2013, *Times Higher Education* reported a memo sent to staff on 10 June by Leicester University's Pro VC Mark Thompson, which began by stating that non-submission is 'clearly an important performance indicator' for Leicester's need to 'reduce to a minimum the number of colleagues who are on teaching and research contracts but are not funded to do research'. For this reason, Thompson continued, the position of eligible staff not submitted to REF 2014 would be reviewed. Unless there were 'extenuating circumstances',[74] such staff might be put on a 'teaching-dominant' contract (provided they could show 'teaching excellence' and a vacancy existed). Alternatively, they might continue on a teaching and research contract but had to meet 'realistic' performance targets within a year. Should those targets not be met, 'the normal consequence would be dismissal on the ground of unsatisfactory performance'.[75] A month later, the *Higher* reported that Niall Piercy, Deputy Dean for Operations at Swansea University's School of Management, had sent out a similar memo informing academic staff that they would be put on teaching-only contracts if they did not have four 3* papers. Exceptions would be made for early-career colleagues and those with 'special circumstances', but otherwise people excluded from the REF could expect to teach up to 18 hours a week (in a school where the normal teaching load had been 6 hours).[76]

To their credit, other universities went out of their way to assure their staff that exclusion from the REF would not have long-term career repercussions. The tone of 'An update on REF selection decisions', posted on the website of

---

[74] One such circumstance was if 'the number of individuals submitted is "constrained" by the volume of case studies their department intends to enter to demonstrate research impact'. A university spokesman denied this 'amounted to game-playing'. Quoted in Paul Jump, 'REF non-submission may have consequences, Leicester warns'. *Times Higher Education*, 8 August 2013.

[75] Paul Jump, 'REF non-submission may have consequences, Leicester warns'.

[76] Paul Jump, 'Swansea's tough REF plans provoke disquiet'. *Times Higher Education*, 5 September 2013.

Goldsmiths College, University of London, on 10 July 2013, could not have been further from these threats. Rather than dismissing 2* research as something that was no longer worth the university's supporting because it no longer brought in QR funding, the Deputy Warden, Professor Jane Powell, stressed that 3* and 4* outputs 'constitute a relatively small proportion of the excellent work produced in any university, with much other work nevertheless being recognised as of international calibre (2*)'. While 'many staff who have produced work which is of high significance to their discipline, and highly valued by Goldsmiths, may not ultimately be included in our submissions to this REF', she continued, 'eventual non-selection at the end of the REF 2014 process does not in itself reflect adversely on the intrinsic importance of a staff member's research, and *will not affect terms and conditions of employment or promotion decisions*'.[77] York University, which took a similar line, went as far as building an assurance that 'Submission to the REF is not considered a criterion for promotion' into its formal promotion procedures.[78]

Elsewhere university managers have been more mealy-mouthed. Following talks with the UCU, Lancaster University assured its staff in the summer of 2014 that

> although it is anticipated that the number of staff submitted to REF2014 will be below the 92% submitted for RAE2008 and not all contractually REF-eligible staff will be submitted ... Career progression of staff will not be affected and there will not be any contractual changes or instigation of *formal* performance management procedures *solely* on the basis of not being submitted for REF2014.[79]

The emphasis on the italicized words is mine. It is difficult to ignore the fact that Leicester University's Pro VC also claimed 'the university stands by its previously agreed "general principle" that non-submission to the REF "will not, *of itself*, mean that there will be negative career repercussions for that person"', even while spelling out his university's intention to review the contractual positions of all non-submitted staff with a view to putting some on teaching-only contracts and firing others. If universities intended that non-submission in the 2014 REF should not in any way negatively affect individuals' career prospects,

---

[77] 'An update on REF selections decisions from Professor Jane Powell'. 10 July 2013. http://www.gold.ac.uk/staff-news/content/10july-ref/ (accessed 2 February 2014). Emphasis added.

[78] University of York, 'Promotion of Academic, Research and Teaching Staff: Procedures and Criteria 2013-14'. http://www.york.ac.uk/media/abouttheuniversity/supportservices/registrar-secretary/promotions/ProceduresCriteria2013-14.pdf (accessed 3 February 2014).

[79] Lancaster University, 'REF Statement'. Emphasis added

what stopped them from saying so unequivocally and unambiguously – as was done at Goldsmiths or York?

In the event, things began to move at Lancaster even before the university had hit the send button on its REF submission. In November 2013 the FASS Dean advised Heads of Department to take responsibility henceforth for the Performance and Development Reviews (PDRs) of all staff not returned in REF 2014 with the aim of ensuring that they will be returned in REF 2020. The PDR, which all Lancaster staff have to undergo annually, is described on the Human Resources website as follows: 'Reviewers and Reviewees should be engaged in discussions *throughout the year* about objectives, performance & development … The formal PDR meeting is a culmination of these regular discussions, drawing together the threads of the ongoing conversations'. In the History Department, PDR reviewer duties had previously been divided among the professoriate on the assumption that this is a form of collegial mentoring rather than a tool of line management. The PDR is legally distinguishable from 'formal performance management', and the relevant policy document is clear that 'the University's Capability & Disciplinary procedures will be used to help manage poor performance'. Nevertheless, the PDR *is* a formal requirement, which the university regards as 'a critical process for enhancing individual and organisational performance'.[80] Using it to police the future research of REFugees (as they have sardonically come to be known in Lancaster) is clearly contrary to the spirit, if not the letter, of the undertakings given to the UCU.

Staff members excluded from Lancaster's REF submission are now being singled out as a group and treated differently *solely as a result of that exclusion*. Unlike their colleagues, whose PDRs will continue to be of the more collegial kind, they will be subject to formal surveillance by their line manager in an objective-setting and monitoring process, the overriding goal of which has become the production of research that can be included in the university's 2020 REF submission. In the History Department, the managerial gaze will fall most attentively on those engaged in interdisciplinary work that engages with contemporary social and cultural theory, because it is they who were disproportionately excluded this time around. The features that made their published articles and chapters so 'difficult to assess', 'unconventional' or 'risky' for REF 2014 will no doubt be the things that the Head of Department will be expected to make easy, conventional and safe for REF 2020 and beyond. It is not only interdisciplinary enquiry, though, whose future is on the line here. In Paolo Palladino's words, this kind of research micromanagement

---

[80] Lancaster University, 'Performance and Development Review (PDR) Policy'. http://www.lancaster.ac.uk/hr/pdr/files/PDRPolicy.pdf (accessed 3 February 2014).

calls into question the meaning of 'academic freedom' not just within Lancaster University, but across British universities more generally ... testing all those of us who still believe that a reflective culture, which universities are supposed to cultivate, is essential to sustaining belief in the possibility of creating a better world.[81]

Individuals' scholarly reputations have been sullied and their confidence dented. Before long, no doubt, the university will follow Trevor McMillan's interview with *Nature* in presenting this substantively (if not formally) disciplinary action as providing 'support' and 'help' to staff members. It is, therefore, all the more important to reiterate that *the procedures used to make the judgements of quality on the basis of which these individuals were excluded from the REF fail to meet all internationally recognized norms of peer review.* Indeed, Lancaster's staff selection process for the REF provides less protection against error or bias than the university gives its students. Not only does Lancaster require an external examiner for a PhD to be 'an experienced member of another university qualified ... to assess the thesis *within its own field'*,[82] but it expects all *undergraduate* work that significantly counts towards a degree to be marked anonymously, moderated or second-marked internally and made available for inspection by an external examiner. Why are those whose livelihood depends on their research – *and its reputation for quality, established through peer-reviewed publications* – not given at least equivalent consideration as the students they supervise and teach? Morally, if not legally, this surely raises issues around the employer's statutory duty of care.

---

[81] Palladino, 'Why the REF is bad for the very idea of the university'.

[82] Lancaster University, 'Examination of Research Degrees: Guidance Notes'. http://www.lancaster.ac.uk/sbs/registry/docs/ExternalExaminers/guidance-notes-research-degree.pdf (accessed 20 April 2014).

4

THE ABJECT ACADEMY

4.1 A 'TOLERABLE PROCESS'? METRICS REVISITED

In a 2013 interview cited earlier, Sir Peter Swinnerton-Dyer, architect of the first UGC research selectivity exercise in 1986, argued that the RAE long since ceased to be a 'tolerable process'. 'The one question a modern civil servant fails to ask', he complains, is 'is it worth the extra effort?' For him the answer is an emphatic no. In particular, evaluation of individual researchers' outputs – the 'silly idea' that has stood at the heart of the RAE since 1989 and been my main focus throughout this book – produces 'an absolutely intolerable level of work'. In his view,

> The rot really set in when vice-chancellors ceased to see the RAE as a funding mechanism and regarded it, instead, as a 'free-standing assessment of research quality,' with the added advantage of being 'useful as a means to get rid of people not doing any research or to make them do more teaching. If that is what vice-chancellors want, they can conduct their own internal processes, but, nationwide, I don't think such an exercise is justified'.[1]

David Eastwood, on the other hand, believed that 'On any impartial assessment, the research assessment exercise has been a success ... Its impact has been profoundly positive'. Not only, he wrote in 2007, did the RAE 'secure research funding by justifying it to a then-sceptical Government', giving 'research-intensive institutions ... the benefit of quality research income (QR) to invest against their priorities', but,

> The RAE has also been *the key instrument for performance management* in institutions, and much of the obloquy that has been heaped on it has arisen from university managements doing what they should do but sheltering behind the

---

[1] Jump, 'Evolution of the REF'.

pretext of the RAE. To this extent, the RAE has done more than drive research quality; *it has been crucial to modernisation.*[2]

Both men are, of course, right. They are just judging by different yardsticks. An older generation of sociologists might have spoken of manifest and latent functions.

Viewed as a mechanism for distributing QR funding, the RAE/REF must be reckoned an inordinately costly and time-consuming way of telling us what we already know (or could have found out in much easier ways, mostly involving the reviled metrics). As I have shown, its 'expert assessments' of individual outputs – the bedrock upon which its profiles of UOAs and universities rest – are anything but trustworthy. They would not pass muster in any other academic context in which peer review is used internationally or even nationally. This is true both of HEFCE's REF panels, where overworked assessors assign vaguely defined grades in fields that are frequently not their own, and of individual universities' staff selection procedures, which frequently satisfy neither HEFCE's criteria of transparency, accountability, consistency and inclusivity nor the normal expectations of academic peer review. If we factor in the opportunity costs of the research that might have been done in the time that has been sacrificed to the REF, not to mention the serious distortions to the research process caused by tailoring work to suit REF priorities and the havoc university staff selection practices have played with collegial relations and faculty members' morale, it seems clear that the exercise has gotten way, way too big for its boots.

Let me at this point introduce some crude, back-of-the-envelope metrics. Eleven British universities made the top 100 in the 2013–2014 *Times Higher Education* World University Rankings. Of these, eight were also in the top 10 in RAE 2008 and the other three in the top 20. The five top-ranked universities in RAE 2008 (Cambridge, Oxford, LSE, Imperial and UCL) were the leading British performers in the THE list, though their rank order differed. Four of the top five universities in RAE 2008 were also the four leading UK representatives in both the QS and Shanghai world university rankings (LSE came in much lower on both lists, but only because it is a specialized school).[3] Only two universities in the RAE top 10 did not make the THE top 100 – Warwick (7th in RAE and 141st in THE) and Essex (9th in RAE and 251–275 in THE). Coincidentally, 14 of the top 15 (and 21 of the top 26) UK universities in the THE rankings are members of the Russell Group, as are 19 of the top 25 universities in RAE 2008. Only one

---

[2] Eastwood, 'Goodbye to the RAE'. Emphasis added.

[3] QS ranks LSE overall at 68, but describes it as 'the world's leading dedicated social science institution'. http://www.topuniversities.com/universities/london-school-economics-political-science-lse/undergrad (accessed 11 February 2014).

Russell Group member failed to make the THE top 200 (Cardiff, 21st in RAE 2008). Conversely, only four universities not in the Russell Group made it into the RAE top 20 (Essex 9th, St Andrew's 12th, Bath 18th and Lancaster 19th), all of which were at the time members of the 1994 Group. Of 31 British universities listed in the THE top 200, just two – Aberdeen at 188th and Dundee at 196th – were in neither the Russell Group nor the 1994 Group.

Though there are occasional outliers – Warwick and Essex at one pole and Cardiff at the other – these are impressive correlations. The universities that performed best in the THE top 200 were overwhelmingly the same universities that dominated the RAE 2008 rankings, and all but two were members of the Russell or 1994 Groups – which as we saw earlier received nearly 85% of QR funding in 2012–2013.[4] Were HEFCE to have distributed QR funding according to the THE rankings, therefore, or simply handed most of it over to the Russell Group and 1994 Group on the common-sense ground that everyone knows that this is where the bulk of UK university research is concentrated, the outcome would not have been very different from that produced by the RAE. Some universities would have improved their positions or slipped in the rankings,[5] but the overall shape of the system (including eight out of the RAE top 10) would look much the same. Only it wouldn't have required 67 'expert panels' spending a year assessing 215,507 books and papers[6] and 60 million quid of taxpayers' money to tell us the blindingly obvious. All those eminent brains – not to mention the departmental Research Directors, Associate Deans for Research, members ad hoc with senior involvement in previous assessment exercises, critical friends, impact champions and all the rest of the local apparatchiks whose numbers have swollen even further in the 2014 REF – could have spent hundreds more hours in the library, the lecture hall or the lab, doing what the public thinks it is paying them to do.

What is most significant about these correlations is that neither membership in the Russell Group nor position in the THE rankings rests on judgements of research *quality* as understood within the discourse of the RAE/REF. Admission to the Russell Group seems to depend upon a number of factors, including size, teaching and links with industry and the public sector, as well as research capacity and performance. Lancaster was not among the 1994 Group

---

[4] See above, pp. 47–8.

[5] We cannot simply assume that the RAE rankings are more accurate and use such discrepancies as an argument for retaining the REF. The discrepancy between the positions of, say, Warwick and Essex – or Cardiff – in the RAE table and other rankings could be seen as evidence for the bias and subjectivity inherent in the RAE/REF process.

[6] The number of outputs submitted to the 2008 RAE. See HEFCE, 'Submissions'.

members invited to defect to the Russell Group in 2012 despite outperforming seven of the group's existing members (and one of its new recruits) in the 2008 RAE. Essex, which also conspicuously failed to secure an invitation to the big boys' club, ranked higher in the RAE than two-thirds of Russell Group universities.[7] RAE performance is not factored into the THE rankings either. Indeed, for all HEFCE's talk of the REF providing 'benchmarking information and reputational yardsticks', none of the three major global university ranking organizations draw on RAE data, preferring to use their own combinations of surveys and metrics. This underlines my earlier point that there may be rather more to 'international benchmarking' than UK academia getting together and unilaterally awarding itself stars.[8]

THE gives 30% of its overall score for 'the learning environment' (i.e. teaching), 7.5% for 'international outlook' and 2.5% for 'industry income'. The remaining 60% is based entirely on research-related measures, of which, the website proudly boasts, 'Our research influence indicator is the flagship. Weighted at 30 per cent of the overall score, it is *the single most influential of the 13 indicators*, and looks at the role of universities in spreading new knowledge and ideas'. The terms in which THE congratulates itself upon its use of citation data could not be further removed from the anti-bibliometrics bombast encountered earlier from all sides of the British academic establishment:

> We examine research influence by capturing *the number of times a university's published work is cited by scholars globally*. This year, our data supplier Thomson Reuters examined more than 50 million citations to 6 million journal articles, published over five years. The data are drawn from the 12,000 academic journals indexed by Thomson Reuters' Web of Science database and include all indexed journals published between 2007 and 2011.

The rest of the THE's research score is derived from research income (6%), 'research output scaled against staff numbers' (6%) and 'a university's reputation for research excellence among its peers, based on the 10,000-plus responses to

---

[7]   Lancaster was 19th in the 2008 RAE rankings, above King's (20), Cardiff (21), Nottingham (22), Birmingham (24), Newcastle (25), Exeter (27) and Liverpool (38). Essex was 9th.

[8]   For *THE* rankings, see below. The Shanghai methodology is explained at http://www.shanghairanking.com/ARWU-Methodology-2013.html and the QS at http://www.topuniversities.com/university-rankings-articles/world-university-rankings/qs-world-university-rankings-methodology (both accessed 12 February 2014).

our annual academic reputation survey' (18%).[9] In contrast to the REF's reliance on UK-based panellists, the latter is available in 10 languages and uses United Nations data to ensure that it reflects the demographics of world scholarship and the spread of academic disciplines. The survey used for the 2013 rankings had 16,639 responses from 144 countries, from respondents who on average had been working in the academy for 17 years. Of these,

> 33 per cent of responses hail from North America, 17 per cent from Western Europe, 12 per cent from East Asia, 10 per cent from Oceania, 6 per cent from Eastern Europe, 5 per cent from South America and 5 per cent from the Middle East.[10]

Some might find it ironic that these rankings should loom so large on British VCs' horizons, given the sector's professed disdain for the quantitative methods upon which their assessments are based. But it is not unreasonable for university administrators to take these tables seriously – or at least, to take them as seriously as they do the RAE/REF. *Despite their differences of methodology, the RAE and the THE come up with remarkably similar rankings.*

Other metrics point to the same conclusion. Drawing on the Web of Science, Dorothy Bishop, Professor of Developmental Neuropsychology at Oxford University, showed a very high correlation (0.84) between the 2008 RAE psychology results and an H-index of citations calculated for departments (rather than individuals). She also had another intriguing, if somewhat embarrassing, finding:

> The one variable that accounted for additional variance in outcome, over and above departmental H-index was whether the department had a representative on the psychology panel: if they did, then the trend was for the department to have a higher ranking than that predicted from the H-index.

She charitably explains this by observing:

> It makes sense that if you are a member of a panel, you will be much more clued up than other people about how the whole process works, and you can use this information to ensure your department's submission is strategically optimal.

---

9 Times Higher Education, 'World University Rankings 2013-2014 methodology'. Emphasis added. Available at http://www.timeshighereducation.co.uk/world-university-rankings/2013-14/world-ranking/methodology (accessed 11 February 2014). Since research output is also measured by papers indexed in the Web of Science, bibliometric data actually account for 36% of the overall THE score.

10 Times Higher Education, 'Rankings methodology: experts recognise these as the best'. Available at http://www.timeshighereducation.co.uk/world-university-rankings/2013/reputation-ranking/methodology (accessed 13 February 2014).

The general camaraderie (and a keenly developed sense, no doubt, of belonging to the inner circles of a disciplinary elite) that one would expect to develop in the course of a year between REF panellists might also have had something to do with it. Professor Bishop concludes that her method:

> is crude and imperfect, and I suspect it would not work for all disciplines – especially those in the humanities. It relies solely on citations, and it's debatable whether that is desirable. But for sciences, it seems to be pretty much measuring whatever the RAE was measuring, and it would seem to be the lesser of various possible evils, with a number of advantages compared to the current system. It is transparent and objective, it would not require departments to decide who they do and don't enter for the assessment, and most importantly, it wins hands down on cost-effectiveness. If we'd used this method instead of the RAE, a small team of analysts armed with Web of Science should be able to derive the necessary data in a couple of weeks to give outcomes that are virtually identical to those of the RAE.[11]

The point here is not that bibliometrics offer superior ways of evaluating the quality (or even the influence) of research. For one thing, the Web of Science does not even index books, which are the premium vehicle of research publication in my own discipline. I fully accept many of the arguments against using citations, journal impact factors or other quantitative indicators as measurements of the quality of any *individual* research output. While a handful of well-cited papers may substantially raise a journal's impact factor, it does not follow that the other papers published in the same journal are of equivalent quality; nor is it always the case that the reason a paper is widely cited is because it makes a major contribution to research. I believe North American tenure and promotion committees can pay too much attention to venue of publication, though it is fair to add that they also make extensive use of peer review as a counterbalance. So long as HEFCE's bibliometrics rely only on the Web of Science, they will always be of limited use at the UOA level, particularly in the humanities (where at the very least they would need supplementing with other indicators of citation). It remains the case, nevertheless, that *at the aggregate level of the university as a whole*, results arrived at using metrics have proven to be extremely reliable *predictors* of RAE performance. The university as a whole, of course, is the relevant unit of analysis, because QR funding goes to universities – not to UOAs, and still less to individual researchers.

---

[11] Dorothy Bishop, 'An alternative to REF2014?' Bishopblog, 26 January 2013. http://deevybee.blogspot.co.uk/2013/01/an-alternative-to-ref2014.html (accessed 11 February 2014).

As any first-year statistics student learns, reliability and validity are not the same thing. If metrics-based measures can produce much the same results as those arrived at through an infinitely more costly, laborious and time-consuming process of 'expert review' of individual outputs, there is a compelling reason to go with the metrics; not because it is necessarily a *valid* measure of anything, but because it as *reliable* as the alternative (whose validity, as the last two chapters have shown, is no less dubious for different reasons) and a good deal more cost-efficient. The benefits for collegiality and staff morale of universities *not* having to decide who to enter or exclude from the REF might be seen as an additional reason for favouring metrics, as Professor Bishop points out. I am sure that if the mandarins at HEFCE put their minds to it, they could come up with a more sophisticated and relevant basket of metrics than either the THE's or Professor Bishop's, which would be capable of meeting many of the standard objections to quantification. But this cost-benefit analysis works only so long as we assume, with Swinnerton-Dyer, that the objective of the REF is to provide a tolerable process for distributing HEFCE's QR budget – and nothing more. Metrics will not allow us to drill down to individuals (or possibly even to UOAs) with any degree of validity, but *they do not need to* if the REF is merely a funding mechanism. Any such additional information – and the time, money and effort spent in gathering it – would be superfluous to what is required.

All of this suggests to me, therefore, that informing QR funding decisions has long since ceased to be the principal objective of the REF. Had it been, appropriate metrics would long ago have been adopted with a big sigh of relief across the sector, leaving us with much more time to get on with doing our research, free of HEFCE's interference. But if we follow David Eastwood in understanding the RAE/REF as a crucial element in the 'modernization' of British universities, the costs and benefits might look rather different. From this point of view the features that disqualify the REF from being a valid exercise in research evaluation according to internationally accepted norms of peer review might just turn out to be what is most important about it. The UK's academic establishment fought a tenacious campaign to retain these idiosyncrasies in the face of not only politicians' pressure to replace the RAE's 'expert review' with metrics, but also persuasive evidence that the outcomes for QR allocations would not have been all that different if they had. This behaviour is inexplicable unless they had some considerable stakes in *the process itself*. It is time, I think, to move from considering what the REF does not do – which is to provide a fair or competent assessment of the originality, rigour and significance of individual scholars' research – to looking at *what it actually does*.

4.2 THE REF AS MORAL REGULATION: BRINGING FOUCAULT BACK HOME

Professor Eastwood may be right that earlier RAEs provided evidence of the vitality of research in British universities at a time when many in Westminster questioned it, as was undoubtedly the case during the Thatcher years. But I am not convinced that subsequent UK governments, of whatever political stripe, have been as sceptical about investing in university research as he would have us believe – especially in the STEM subjects. Humanities research has always been more difficult to defend in utilitarian terms because whatever benefits it has are less immediately measurable or demonstrable. Politicians do generally want to see evidence of value for money, which is a slightly different matter. If anything, the last-minute inclusion of a 20% weighting for impact in REF 2014 (which is scheduled to rise to 25% or more in REF 2020) suggests that previous RAEs failed to satisfy whatever doubts they had on that score. In any case, would governments not have been just as open to persuasion by a case based on metrics, which was the Treasury's preference back in 2006 and remains the currency of DBIS's reports on the health of the UK's research base?[12] It is sceptical academics that Eastwood is trying to convince here, not politicians. Without HEFCE's umbrella, he implies, things would be much worse. The RAE/REF is an offer nobody who values public funding of research can refuse.

But Eastwood's other arguments give the game away, even if we have to unpack the substance of what he is saying from the anodyne technocratic language in which he wraps it. National research assessments, he maintains, not only provided 'the bedrock of the case for investment in a high-quality research base', but also became 'a driver of [that] globally competitive research base'. Indeed, the RAE 'has done more than drive research quality'. It has become '*the key instrument for performance management* in institutions'.[13] What Swinnerton-Dyer regarded as the moment when 'the rot really set in' is for Eastwood the real point of the exercise. Whatever the original intent of the RAE, its lasting value is as what I shall call an apparatus of moral regulation. By this I understand (as Philip Corrigan and I defined the concept back in 1985 in our book *The Great Arch*) 'a project of normalizing, rendering natural, taken for granted, in a word "obvious", what are in fact ontological and epistemological premises of a particular and historical form of social order'.[14] Eastwood prefers to talk of

---

[12] See above, p. 40.

[13] Eastwood, 'Goodbye to the RAE'. Emphasis added.

[14] Philip Corrigan and Derek Sayer, *The Great Arch: English State Formation and Cultural Revolution*. Oxford: Blackwell, 1985, 4.

the RAE as 'crucial to modernisation', but it comes down to the same thing. Like 'improvement' in an earlier moment of British state formation, the term is freighted with moral ballast.[15] Who, other than Luddites, reactionaries and other enemies of progress, could possibly not want to become *modern*?

Especially, it might be added, when modernization inflates the value of your own office to £372,000 p.a., which is the basic salary that Eastwood received in 2011–2012 as Vice-Chancellor of Birmingham University. He took up the post in 2009, after his three-year stint at HEFCE. At the time this was the highest salary paid to any VC in the land. It was four times what the most senior professors in UK universities were then earning and more than eight times the average full-time British academic salary.[16] If mention of Professor Eastwood's compensation is thought *ad hominem*, I could well respond: but so is the REF. It became particularly personal in universities like Leicester and Swansea that took HEFCE's defunding of 2* research as a reason to begin threatening colleagues whose published, peer-reviewed research did not pass their Star Chamber assessments with dismissal.[17] The point is not an irrelevant sideswipe. Eastwood is one of the architects[18] of a revolution in higher education that in Britain, as in the United States, has led to a huge rise in numbers of senior administrators – each with their entourage of what Benjamin Ginsberg has christened deanlings and deanlets – relative to academics as well as growing discrepancies between their respective

---

[15] See Corrigan and Sayer, *The Great Arch*, Chapter 6.

[16] Eastwood was 2nd in total remuneration (£406,000) after Andrew Hamilton at Oxford (£424,000). That year the average professorial salary at Birmingham was £79,622 and the average academic salary £47,792. UK averages were £76,214 and £47,609, respectively. Jack Grove, 'Higher Education Pay Survey, 2013'. *Times Higher Education*, 28 March 2013. At the time of writing, Eastwood's salary (of £400,000 pa) remains the highest in the UK. Richard Garner, '"The academic fat cats: Vice-chancellors at Britain's top universities get £22,000 pay rises – as lecturers are stuck on 1 per cent'. *The Independent*, 2 January 2014.

[17] See above, p. 79.

[18] In addition to his service at HEFCE and Birmingham, Eastwood has been VC at the University of East Anglia and Chief Executive of AHRB (the predecessor of AHRC). He is currently Chair of the Russell Group, a Director of Universities Superannuation Scheme (USS), a Board Member of Universities UK (UUK), a member of AHRC and a member of the Advisory Board of the Higher Education Policy Institute (HEPI). He has previously served on the Roberts review, the Tomlinson Group on 14-19 Education and the Quality Assurance Agency (QAA) Board, as well as chairing the QAA Steering Group for Benchmarking, the Association of the Universities of the East of England, the 1994 Group and UUK's Longer Term Strategy Group. He was also a member of the Browne review. University of Birmingham, 'Vice-Chancellor's Profile'. http://www.birmingham.ac.uk/university/welcome/vcprofile.aspx (accessed 22 February 2014).

salaries.[19] I draw attention to this differential less because I find it morally reprehensible – though I do – than as an index of shifting power relations within the academy and a measure of how today's managers value their own contribution by comparison with that of teachers and researchers. Even Business Secretary Vince Cable and Universities Minister David Willetts, who are generally pretty relaxed about people getting filthy rich so long as they pay their taxes,[20] felt compelled to state in their funding letter to HEFCE for 2014–2015: 'We are very concerned about the substantial upward drift of salaries of some top management'.[21]

If we ask the question 'What does the REF do?' in these terms and against this background, the answer is – rather a lot. Like all forms of state regulation the REF is an apparatus of empowerment (of some) and subordination (of others). Most obviously, it provides university managers with comprehensive data on the research performance of their own and other institutions and units within them upon which they can plan and act. It is easy to map REF findings directly on to the university, since UOA boundaries will in many cases broadly coincide with those of academic departments. The data are sufficiently standardized to permit comparisons across the institution ('Are we getting as good a bang for our bucks in Chemistry as in Economics?') and relative to competitors ('Has our investment in Linguistics paid off in terms of an improved ranking vis-à-vis universities X, Y and Z?'). Even if the scores given to individual researchers and outputs are not made public, enough information is provided to identify departmental strengths and weaknesses, particularly since profiles replaced aggregate scores in RAE 2008. It will be clear which bits of a UOA ranking derive from outputs, environment and impact, and – crucially – what proportions of its outputs fall into the precious 3* and 4* bands.

Swinnerton-Dyer's view that performance management is a matter for individual VCs only underlines how radically UK higher education has changed since the 1980s. No single university would have the resources – let alone the authority, which is that of the state itself – to generate such comprehensive findings. Nor would any merely local appraisal carry the same weight, because it is the fact that this is a *national* exercise carried out under the watchful eye of a *public*

---

[19] See Benjamin Ginsberg, *The Fall of the Faculty: The Rise of the All-Administrative University and Why It Matters.* New York: Oxford University Press, 2011.

[20] I allude, of course, to a remark made by Cable's predecessor Peter Mandelson – which should serve to remind us that the revolution in UK higher education I am discussing here was carried through as much under Labour as under the auspices of the Tories.

[21] 'Funding for higher education in England for 2014-15: HEFCE grant letter from BIS'. http://www.hefce.ac.uk/news/newsarchive/2014/name,85409,en.html (accessed 12 February 2014).

body that gives REF scores their clout. Whether it is true or not, the claim is that every department has been rigorously evaluated against every other department in the country and all outputs judged by disciplinary experts against international benchmarks. This is a powerful repertoire of legitimation; one against which it is difficult to argue without appearing to engage in special pleading. The very laboriousness of the process – the whole theatrical panoply of Main Panels and subpanels, consultation exercises and pilot studies, the endlessly revised and constantly updated procedural guidelines, the forms and templates, the census dates and submission deadlines, the equality assessments and the final reports on the state of the disciplines – is an earnest of its high seriousness. The rituals of the REF punctuate British academic life, lending a stately pomp and circumstance to what might otherwise be seen as no more than a vulgar bit of bean counting – even if at the end of the day, many of us can see (but are too cowed, cowardly or self-interested to admit) that the emperor has no clothes.

Armed with the information provided by HEFCE's research assessment exercises, university managers can synchronize resource allocation decisions – closing, merging or investing in departments, for example – to the REF cycle, planning for the future. As Eastwood observed, not only are many of the economic costs of performance appraisal thereby deflected on to HEFCE, but also much of the force of any resulting opprobrium. Before Eastwood became its VC, Birmingham University caused outrage when it closed the Centre for Contemporary Cultural Studies in 2002 despite high student demand and an international reputation enjoyed by few other units in the university. Many suspected the decision was politically motivated: the CCCS had been a persistent critic of Birmingham's management since the 1960s as well as the source of a string of influential critical analyses of contemporary British society and culture that brought the university a notoriety its administrators might rather have done without. But the university was able to defend its decision – together with other 'restructuring' – with reference to the Centre's poor showing in the 2001 RAE.[22] Instead of Birmingham having to justify what much of the academic world saw as an act of intellectual vandalism, the onus was on opponents of closure to show why scarce resources should continue to be poured into an underperforming unit. It is but a small step from there for management to insinuate – as Adam Tickell would 10 years later, speaking now on behalf of David Eastwood's Birmingham – that researchers whose outputs do not score at least 3* in the REF are not pulling their weight.

---

[22] See Polly Curtis, 'Birmingham's cultural studies department given the chop'. *Guardian*, 22 June 2002; Adam Fox, 'The wrong result'. *Guardian*, 17 July 2002; Polly Curtis, 'Cultural elite express opposition to Birmingham closure'. *Guardian*, 18 July 2002.

Behind the old-fashioned collegial facade of readings by expert panel-lists, the RAE/REF regime establishes – *and enforces* – a new understanding of research, which allows the activities of individual academics to be brought under an unprecedented degree of institutional scrutiny and control. In a dim and distant past that is not entirely imaginary (and still survives for the shrinking minority of tenured faculty members in North America), research was some-thing that academics undertook as a regular part of their job, like teaching. In the normal course of events, research would lead to publication, which would in turn provide the basis for career advancement along the lines discussed in Chapter 1. Universities generally expected their staff to publish (though in pre-RAE Britain, unlike in contemporary North America, few of them policed that expectation) and academics expected their universities to give them sufficient time to pursue their research. For this reason, bargaining on being offered a job would invariably involve discussion of teaching loads. Unless people got exter-nal grants, there was no *specific* funding for time spent on research, but the understanding, on both sides, was that the salary was meant to support and remunerate a staff member's research as well as his or her teaching. Conversely, while universities had a general reputational interest in faculty members pub-lishing – preferably in the best places – they had no reason to seek to *manage* individuals' research as part of any wider departmental or institutional plan.

In this pre-RAE world, Adam Tickell's claim that 'half the work Birmingham submitted to the 2008 research assessment exercise was unfunded' would have been quite literally meaningless. It would have made no sense because there was no direct link between faculty members' *individual* research and publica-tions and *university* funding. Unless it was supported by a grant, the research undertaken by academic staff was either all unfunded or all funded, depending on whether or not you regarded salary as including compensation for time spent on research. Most people would have seen the latter as an entirely scho-lastic question, akin to asking how many angels can dance on a pinhead, if they thought about it at all. When I returned to the UK in 2006 after 20 years work-ing in North America, I was nonplussed when an administrator at Lancaster started musing aloud about whether the university could 'afford' to have aca-demic staff doing 'unfunded' research. I still think it an utterly philistine posi-tion for a senior manager to take in any university with pretensions to being 'internationally significant',[23] but I now understand the reasoning behind it. This perverted calculus is made possible by – *indeed it is demanded by* – the

---

[23] This is Lancaster's latest version of its official aspiration, which is intended to replace the earlier 1/10/100 mantra (#1 in the North West, in the top 10 in the UK and in the top 100 globally). Not being measurable, it is also less deniable.

RAE/REF regulatory regime. Because the only government support for universities' 'research infrastructure and … pathbreaking research in keeping with their own mission' comes through QR funding and QR funding is tied to RAE/REF rankings, any research that scores below a 3* necessarily appears as unfunded.

The accomplishment of the RAE/REF – if we want to call it that – is to have made research *accountable* in the literal sense of turning it into a possible object of monetary calculation. This makes the REF a disciplinary technology in Foucault's sense of the term, which works above all through the self-policing that is produced by the knowledge that one's activities are the subject of constant oversight.[24] Both inputs (including, crucially, academics' time) and outputs (as evaluated by the REF panels and monetized by the QR funding formula) can now be *costed*. The corollary is that activities that do not generate revenues, whether in the form of research grants or QR income, may not count in the university's eyes as research at all. It does not necessarily follow from this that universities will seek to 'reduce to a minimum the number of colleagues who are on teaching and research contracts but not funded to do research', as Pro-VC Mark Thompson wanted to do at Leicester,[25] or even that they will endeavour to manage individuals' research so as to maximize their chances of future REF submission, as the FASS is attempting to do at Lancaster. But even if, as at Goldsmiths, a university recognizes that research that does not bring in QR funding may still be of considerable benefit to the institution and the researcher's discipline, that research will appear in the loss rather than the income column in the university's accounts. It becomes an activity subsidized by the more profitable portions of the enterprise. I choose my words carefully here. Though the university is not a corporation, the allocation of QR funding through the REF constrains it to act like one, if only to secure the resources upon which its academic mission depends. VCs begin to think of themselves as CEOs, wearing their lanyards like bizarre chains of office and paying themselves accordingly. What we have here is a classic case of Weberian rationalization.[26]

And there is, as readers of Max Weber might expect, a substantive irrationality (as he would have called it) at its very heart. The logic of discovery and the logic of accountancy can often pull in very different directions, and discovery frequently involves serendipity and risk. It cannot be ordered like

---

[24] See inter alia Michel Foucault, *Discipline and Punish: The Birth of the Prison*. New York: Vintage, 1995.

[25] See above, p. 79.

[26] I elaborate on Max Weber's notion of rationalization in Derek Sayer, *Capitalism and Modernity: An Excursus on Marx and Weber*. London: Routledge, 1990, Chapter 4.

pizza or booked in advance like a vacation. There are no guaranteed returns on investments. Ludwig Wittgenstein, who is arguably the most important philosopher of the 20th century, would undoubtedly have fared poorly under the post-1986 UK academic regime since he published only one book, the *Tractatus Logico-Philosophicus*, in his lifetime – and that was several years before his appointment in Cambridge. In several of the universities examined here, so dismal a performance would have risked dismissal, or at the least transfer to a teaching-only contract. Peter Higgs, winner of the 2013 Nobel Prize in Physics for his 1964 prediction of the Higgs Boson particle, has recently confessed that he was 'an embarrassment to [his] department when they did research assessment exercises' and would likely have been fired by Edinburgh University had he not been nominated for the Nobel in 1980. He is almost certainly correct in thinking that 'no university would employ him in today's academic system because he would not be considered "productive" enough'.

What is still more disturbing – at least to anybody who cares about the future of research in British universities – is that Higgs is probably equally right to doubt that 'a similar breakthrough could be achieved in today's academic culture, because of the expectations on academics to collaborate and keep churning out papers'.[27] 'No-one wanted to work with me', he says, because he was considered 'a bit of a crank'.[28] Interviewed en route to collect his Nobel Prize in Stockholm, he told the *Guardian*: 'It's difficult to imagine how I would ever have enough peace and quiet in the present sort of climate to do what I did in 1964'.[29] The tragedy is that university managers and their minions at lower levels in the hierarchy, eager to advance their own careers by doing whatever authority asks of them, may very well not care. The system does not reward them for taking intellectual risks (or encouraging their junior colleagues to do so). As Peter Scott, Professor of Higher Education Studies at London University's Institute of Education (and a former VC of Kingston University and editor of the *Times Higher Education Supplement*) succinctly explains:

> These days, universities' main objective is to achieve better REF grades, not to produce excellent science and scholarship. This has become a subsidiary goal that only matters to the extent that it delivers top grades. *Research is reduced to*

---

[27] Decca Aitkenhead, 'Peter Higgs: I wouldn't be productive enough for today's academic system'. *Guardian*, 6 December 2013.

[28] Jim Al-Khalilli, 'Peter Higgs on fame and the boson that bears his name'. BBC radio interview, 13 February 2014. http://www.bbc.co.uk/blogs/radio4/posts/Peter-Higgs-on-the-Higgs-Boson-the-Large-Hadron-Collider-and-fame (accessed 16 April 2014).

[29] Quoted in Aitkenhead, 'Peter Higgs'.

what counts for the REF. Four 'outputs' over five years need to be submitted, so the temptation to recycle rather than create is very strong. Big ideas don't come to annual order. Only the genius or the fool would dare to submit many fewer, even if their research office agreed. REF outputs also need to be ground-breaking, not world-shattering. To be too ahead of the curve of received wisdom is risky, especially outside the 'objective' sciences – ideas that are too risky can be dismissed as silly. The REF is designed to pick present, not future winners.[30]

There is a surreal footnote to this cautionary tale. *Physics Letters,* a respected international journal published by CERN in Switzerland – the folks whose Large Hadron Collider would eventually prove Higgs right about his boson – rejected his breakthrough 1964 paper on the grounds that it was 'of no obvious relevance to physics'.[31] As I said earlier, experts in a field are not always the people most capable of spotting excellence, especially when the work in question genuinely is original. Fortunately, it was still a free academic world back then and Higgs was not submitting his work to an REF subpanel (or a university's internal evaluation) in which a single reviewer's decision could be the last word on the subject. *Physical Review Letters,* the leading US physics journal, published 'Broken Symmetries and the Masses of Gauge Bosons' later that year. Had there been an REF then, I wonder which way the panel's 'expert' grading would have gone? Would it have been a 4* – or an unclassified? Assuming, that is, that Dr Higgs's university had included so risky and unconventional a paper, on the merits of which the reviewers clearly disagreed, in its REF submission at all.

4.3 NEOLIBERALISM AND OLD CORRUPTION: A VERY BRITISH BARGAIN

Britain's research assessment exercises are the product of a particular historical moment in the development of a unique university system, which differs in significant ways from those of both North America and continental Europe. Unlike the United States, Britain has no important private universities and only Cambridge (£4.9bn) and Oxford (£3.7bn) have endowments of over £1bn. In 2012, Harvard's endowment fund stood at $30.7bn, Yale's at $19.2bn and Princeton's at $17.4bn, while the average endowment for the 10 richest US schools (two of which are public universities, the University of Michigan and Texas A&M) was $13bn.[32] In 2013, 82 schools in the United States and Canada

---

[30] Scott, 'Why research assessment is out of control'. Emphasis added.

[31] Ian Sample, 'The god of small things'. *Guardian,* 16 November 2007.

[32] Devon Haynie, 'Universities With the Largest Financial Endowments'. *US News,* 1 October 2013.

had endowments of over $1bn, which funded on average 16.2% of their operating budgets.[33] Support for North American universities also comes from state or provincial (as distinct from federal) governments. Most institutions rely on a plurality of income streams, blurring any clear-cut division between public and private. A private university like Harvard attracts huge federal research dollars from agencies like NSF and NEH, while the Bill & Melinda Gates Foundation and the Michael & Susan Dell Foundation provided most of the funding for the computer science complex at the (public) University of Texas at Austin. The relative financial security of major North American research universities sustains a degree of institutional autonomy that their UK equivalents can only envy.

With the partial exception of Oxford and Cambridge, most British universities are for all practical purposes dependents on a single funder, and that funder is the national state. All of their principal sources of income – including domestic student fees,[34] RCUK grants, QR funding and such support for teaching as is still offered by HEFCE – come directly or indirectly from the public purse. This dependency has made them significantly more amenable to centralized direction – and arguably correspondingly more vulnerable to political pressure – than their North American counterparts. This is not (just) because he who pays the piper calls the tune: as we saw, the politicians did not get their way on metrics, though – in a typically British compromise – they forced the academics to give impact a much greater role in the REF than most of the latter would have wished. What is more important is rather *the nature of the regulatory machinery this financial dependency creates*. Because we are dealing with public money, there are pressures for accountability as to how it is spent – including

---

[33] National Association of College and University Business Officers and Commonfund Institute, *2013 NACUBO-Commonfund Study of Endowments*, 1, 4. http://www. nacubo.org/Documents/EndowmentFiles/2013NCSEPressReleaseFinal.pdf (accessed 15 April 2014).

[34] To clarify, *The Independent Review of Higher Education Funding and Student Finance*, better known as the Browne Report, was published on 20 October 2010. Its main recommendations – that caps on student fees and admissions quotas for individual universities be lifted to allow a free market to develop among educational providers – were substantially accepted by the Coalition government. The report can be downloaded in full at http://www.delni.gov.uk/browne-report-student-fees. Even though the Browne reforms have changed the form in which government channels support for teaching into universities, the state still picks up the tab through its provision of student loans. All accepted students are guaranteed loans and the Student Loan Company (which is state owned) pays tuition directly to the university on the student's behalf. The change may result in the new system costing the state *more* than the old: see John Morgan, '"Massive" budget hole predicted as RAB charge rises'. *Times Higher Education*, 21 March 2014.

demands for fairness and transparency on the part of the universities themselves, who are all competing for a share of the same pot. Because funding
operates through the national state, the resulting regulatory machinery is
national in scope, enforcing uniform requirements on all institutions that seek
support from HEFCE and the other funding councils. Stir the British liking for
bureaucracy into the mix (I have to fill out a health and safety risk assessment
before taking a class of young adults to a local museum) and we have a rec-
ipe for a degree of state oversight of universities that many North American
academics would regard as a gross intrusion on institutional autonomy and
individual academic freedom.

Unlike in continental European higher education systems, however, where
the *dirigisme* is upfront and academics are often legally civil servants, in the UK
regulation is mostly exercised through quangos – 'arm's length' bodies that
are not formally part of the state but are funded by public money and perform
governmental functions. In the higher education sector these are largely staffed
by academics. HEFCE and the research councils are listed on the DBIS website
as 'executive non-departmental public bodies' with which DBIS 'works' (so is
the Student Loan Company).[35] We have seen the crucial role HEFCE plays in
allocating funding for research. Since 1993 it has also set admission quotas for
every university in the land, financially penalizing institutions that 'over-recruit'
(though at the time of writing, this is scheduled to end in 2015 as a corollary of the Browne reforms).[36] All applicants for undergraduate courses must go
through another central body, the Universities and Colleges Admissions Service
(UCAS), which limits the number of courses for which they may apply and offers
they may hold. Meanwhile, the Quality Assurance Agency for Higher Education
(QAA), which reports to HEFCE, reviews each university every six years, produc-
ing 'a thorough evaluation of the institution's educational provision' set out in
'a published report that makes judgements and recommendations about academic standards and quality, as well as highlighting good practice'.[37] Thomas
Docherty argues that the QAA process

> confounds a concern for standards (meaning quality) with a demand for stand-
> ardisation (assured by quantity-measurement); and this drives the sector steadily
> towards homogenisation … In this lowest-common-denomination validation,

---

[35] https://www.gov.uk/government/organisations (accessed 8 March 2014).

[36] See John Morgan, 'Undergraduate numbers cap "to be abolished" – Osborne'. *Times Higher Education*, 5 December 2013.

[37] QAA, 'Institutional review'. http://www.qaa.ac.uk/InstitutionReports/types-of-review/ IRENI/Pages/default.aspx (accessed 8 March 2014).

QAA accreditation steadily drives towards mediocrity, endangering actual quality work while singing its official praises.[38]

This is exactly how, I have argued, the REF also operates to undermine the
very standards it purports to be benchmarking.

Such homogenization across the higher education sector is reinforced by a
single national pension scheme (USS) for all UK academics and a single national
pay scale that covers all university employees, including non-academic as well
as academic staff, below the rank of full professor. The Universities and Colleges
Employers Association (UCEA), representing all universities, negotiates pay set-
tlements annually with the University and College Union (UCU), which has the
sole right to bargain collectively on academics' behalf. The product of a 2006
merger between the Association of University Teachers (AUT) and the National
Association of Teachers in Further and Higher Education (NATFHE), UCU claims
to be 'the largest post-school union in the world: a force working for educa-
tors and education that employers and the government cannot ignore'.[39] But
strength in numbers may not be everything. Arguably the inclusion of staff in
further education[40] undermines the union's ability to represent the *distinctive*
interests of university faculty – which above all include their research activities
– and does little to encourage a sense of professional identity and pride of the
sort fostered by The Law Society or the British Medical Association. While the
union staunchly defends national pay bargaining as 'the most efficient way
to agree pay and conditions', avoiding 'more local resources expended, more
local inequality, more local disputes and less stability in the academic labour
market',[41] such a system also clearly limits institutions' ability to compete for
top faculty by offering attractive compensation packages.

Stefan Collini may be right to fear that the Browne reforms spell the beginning of the end of this *ancien régime*,[42] presaging something even worse, but
in its *present* form the UK higher education system bears more resemblance to
Soviet-style planning, in which nominally independent 'enterprises' negotiated

---

[38] Thomas Docherty, 'The Unseen Academy'. *Times Higher Education*, 10 November
2011. See also his books *The English Question, or Academic Freedoms*, Eastbourne:
Sussex Academic Press, 2007, and *For the University: Democracy and the Future of the
Institution*, London: Bloomsbury Academic, 2011.

[39] 'About UCU'. http://www.ucu.org.uk/1685 (accessed 16 April 2014).

[40] Roughly equivalent to continuing education in North America.

[41] 'National pay bargaining essential for equitable sector, says UCU'. 5 July 2007.
http://www.ucu.org.uk/index.cfm?articleid=2671#2100 (accessed 16 April 2014).

[42] Stefan Collini, 'Sold Out'. *London Review of Books*, Vol. 35 No. 20, 24 October 2013.

quotas with ministries, than to anything dreamed up by Friedrich Hayek or Milton Friedman.[43] Certainly, both Conservative and Labour governments' attempts to improve the UK's international competitiveness in the 'knowledge economy' have affected the allocation of resources to universities, including the inclusion of impact in the REF. Corporate styles of line management have displaced collegial self-governance, reducing university senates to little more than echo chambers, and business jargon has taken up robust residence in university boardrooms. The rhetoric of financial accounting, of the sort mobilized by Adam Tickell and Mark Thompson, has become integral to academic decision-making – even if the coin in which the calculations are made bears the same relation to real pricing as the REF does to real peer review. But none of this yet makes British universities independent corporations competing with one another in a genuine market. They are not free to establish their own admissions policies, fee levels and salary scales or to validate their own curricula, except within the narrow limits circumscribed by a multiplicity of state agencies. Ironically, it is the *centralization* of the system that made it so easy for politicians to impose their neoliberal ideological agendas on universities in the first place – beginning with Margaret Thatcher's abolition of tenure under the Education Reform Act of 1988. Eastwood's 'modernization' was orchestrated *by and through the machinery of state.*

The primary instrument through which that modernization was implemented, the quango, might be seen as a latter-day successor to those panels of 'country gentlemen commissioned by the king … to keep the peace of the shire' that the historian F. W. Maitland, talking of justices of the peace, long ago identified as the quintessential English state form.[44] Inherent in such forms is a trade-off of independence from government for the promise of influence within it. As two-way transmission belts between the state and universities, HEFCE and other education quangos represent the locality to the centre and the centre to the locality. This is an enormously strategic position, which confers power and authority on its occupants *both* as representatives of the universities *and* as agents of the state (and allows them frequently to play off one against the other, in ways that are well exemplified in the manoeuvrings that gave the 2014 REF its final form). It is in this buffer zone between individual institutions

---

[43] For a fuller exploration of this parallel, see Ron Amann, 'A Sovietological view of modern Britain'. *Political Quarterly* 74 (2003), 468–480. Annan was Chief Executive of ESRC from 1994–1999.

[44] F. W. Maitland, *The Constitutional History of England.* New York: The Lawbook Exchange (reprint of 1908 edition), 2001, 209. Corrigan and I developed this argument at length in *The Great Arch.*

and the central state, I believe, that the British academic establishment has set up its camp, commandeering the machinery that speaks for and regulates the sector as a whole. It has been moderately successful in keeping the politicians at bay, though at the cost of some questionable compromises. But it has also determinedly used the powers conferred by HEFCE and other quangos to protect its own sectional interests.

The huge changes in UK higher education over the last 30 years – including the abolition of tenure and the binary system, replacement of student maintenance grants by ever-escalating tuition fees and loans and mushrooming participation in post-secondary education – have done little to disturb the hegemony of the country's traditional academic elites: the Oxbridge and London 'golden triangle' and the Russell Group continue to rule the roost, with the remnants of the 1994 Group desperately clinging to their coat tails. These elites have recently been supportive of post-Browne deregulation – on the model, perhaps, of the party and state functionaries who transformed themselves into business oligarchs following the collapse of the Soviet Union. Members of the same schools dominate the major learned societies and professional associations. Nowhere has this hegemony been more apparent than in the rankings produced by successive RAEs, which not only result in the lion's share of QR funding going to Russell and 1994 Group schools, but also advantage applicants from the same universities in competitions for the larger funds available from the research councils and other agencies (since the latter factor quality of the research environment into their funding decisions). This outcome should not surprise us, given the composition of RAE/REF panels and the way in which they are chosen. As I argued in Chapter 2, the REF is tailor-made for the self-replication and legitimation of established hierarchies and networks.

It is the expectations of *these* academic elites that the REF panels and sub-panels, deliberating behind closed doors and shredding their notes, impose on their respective disciplinary fiefs – all without reference to the judgement of the international academic community as expressed in venue of publication, citations, book reviews or any other publicly available medium or form. The REF's handpicked national panels are judge, jury and executioner on the international standing of the UK's research outputs, and there is no appeal against their rankings. Why would anybody even consider giving up such power – which is in effect the power to rig the rules of the game to their perpetual advantage? *What ties the British academic establishment so strongly to the REF's seemingly arcane and cumbersome procedures is self-interest.* Research assessment exercises have been perhaps *the* key means of maintaining establishment domination over the sector. The academic great and good are well aware that the alternative of metrics is likely to be attractive to politicians (of all parties) on grounds of cheapness, simplicity and transparency. E. P. Thompson once urged students of British history to take William Cobbett's notion of 'Old Corruption' – the corruption not of individuals but of an entire parasitic class that uses the machinery of state to protect its collective power and privilege – more seriously as an analytic category.[45] Nowhere does this ancient trope of British political culture have greater contemporary purchase, I would suggest, than with regard to the REF.

But there are less costly ways of evaluating institutions for the purposes of fairly allocating research funding, and it should not be the job of the state to micromanage universities or keep academic elites in power. Whatever this charade may be, it is not a framework for research excellence. The 2014 REF should be the last.

---

[45] See E. P. Thompson, 'The Peculiarities of the English', in *The Socialist Register 1965*. London: Merlin, 311-362. Available at: https://www.marxists.org/archive/thompson-ep/1965/english.htm (accessed 12 August 2014).

BIBLIOGRAPHY

Academic Ranking of World Universities (Shanghai rankings) (2013) Available at: http://www.shanghairanking.com/ARWU2013.html (accessed 15 March 2014).

Academic Ranking of World Universities (Shanghai rankings) (2013) Methodology. Available at: http://www.shanghairanking.com/ARWU-Methodology-2013.html (accessed 15 March 2014).

Aitkenhead D (2013) Peter Higgs: I wouldn't be productive enough for today's academic system. *Guardian*, 6 December.

Al-Khalilli J (2014) Peter Higgs on fame and the boson that bears his name. BBC radio interview. Available at: http://www.bbc.co.uk/blogs/radio4/posts/Peter-Higgs-on-the-Higgs-Boson-the-Large-Hadron-Collider-and-fame (accessed 13 February 2014).

Amann R (2003) A sovietological view of modern Britain. *Political Quarterly* 74 (4) 468-80.

American Association of University Professors (nd) Tenure. Available at: http://www.aaup.org/issues/tenure (accessed 20 December 2013).

Anon (2006) Budget surprise signals research funding revamp. *Times Higher Education*, 24 March.

Anon (2007) Excluding the many for the sake of the few. *Times Higher Education*, 2 February.

Anon (2008) Burning questions for the RAE panels. *Times Higher Education*, 24 April.

Anon (2008) Lancaster produces alternative RAE 2008 rankings. *Times Higher Education*, 18 December.

Anon (2013) The greater good. *Nature* (editorial), 30 December.

Anon (2014) Turkey lifts Twitter ban after court ruling. *Guardian*, 3 April.

Bishop D (2013) An alternative to REF2014? In: Bishopblog. Available at: http://deevybee.blogspot.co.uk/2013/01/an-alternative-to-ref2014.html (accessed 26 January 2013).

Cantor B (2008) How can we measure the quality of research without quantity data? *Times Higher Education*, 11 December.

Churchill W (1947) House of Commons speech, 11 November. Available at: http://hansard.millbanksystems.com/commons/1947/nov/11/parliament-bill (accessed 8 August 2014).

Coles P (2014) The apparatus of research assessment is driven by the academic publishing industry and has become entirely self-serving. In: LSE Blogs, 14 May 2014. Available at: http://blogs.lse.ac.uk/impactofsocialsciences/2013/05/14/the-apparatus-of-research-assessment-is-driven-by-the-academic-publishing-industry/ (accessed 24 February 2014).

Collini S (2013) Sold out. *London Review of Books* 35(20): 3–12.

Corbyn Z (2007) Exclusions from RAE see steep rise. *Times Higher Education*, 2 November.

Corbyn Z (2008) Almost 200 academic staff fight against RAE exclusion. *Times Higher Education*, 7 August.

Corbyn Z (2008) Assessors face 'drowning' as they endeavour to read 2,363 submissions. *Times Higher Education*, 17 April.

Corbyn Z (2008) DIUS abandons plans for different REF systems to judge sciences and arts. *Times Higher Education*, 24 April.

Corbyn Z (2008) Keep peer review at REF core, chairs warn. *Times Higher Education*, 28 August.

Corbyn Z (2008) Launch of REF to be delayed a year. *Times Higher Education*, 10 April.

Corbyn Z (2008) Number of staff entered for RAE rises by 12%. *Times Higher Education*, 31 January.

Corbyn Z (2008) Panels ordered to shred all RAE records. *Times Higher Education*, 17 April.

Corbyn Z (2008) Plans for RAE metrics draw fire from research councils. *Times Higher Education*, 28 February.

Corbyn Z (2008) REF consultation: academe's concerns. *Times Higher Education*, 14 May.

Corbyn Z (2009) Hefce backs off citations in favour of peer review in REF. *Times Higher Education*, 18 June.

Corbyn Z (2009) Impact may account for 30% of researchers' marks in REF. *Times Higher Education*, 23 July.

Corbyn Z (2009) It's evolution, not revolution for REF. *Times Higher Education*, 24 September.

Corbyn Z (2009) RAE sequel looks strangely familiar. *Times Higher Education*, 23 September.

Corbyn Z (2009) Structural adjustments. *Times Higher Education*, 14 May.

Corrigan P and Sayer D (1985) *The Great Arch: English State Formation and Cultural Revolution*. Oxford: Blackwell.

Curtis P (2002) Birmingham's cultural studies department given the chop. *Guardian*, 22 June.

Curtis P (2002) Cultural elite express opposition to Birmingham closure. *Guardian*, 18 July.

Danchev A (2007) Goodbye to the RAE … and hello to the REF. *Times Higher Education*, 30 November.

Department of Business, Innovation and Skills (DBIS) (2013) *International comparative performance of the UK Research Base – 2013*. A report prepared by Elsevier for the Department of Business, Education and Skills. Available at: https://www.gov.uk/government/uploads/system/uploads/attachment_data/file/263729/bis-13-1297-international-comparative-performance-of-the-UK-research-base-2013.pdf (accessed 8 August 2014).

Department for Education and Skills (DES) (2007) *Dfes consultation on the reform of higher education research assessment and funding: summary of responses*. Available at: http://www3.imperial.ac.uk/planning/strategicprojects/researchassessment/future ofresearchassessment (accessed 8 August 2014).

Department for Employment and Learning (2010) *Independent review of higher education funding and student finance*. Browne Report, 2010. Available at: http://www.delni.gov.uk/browne-report-student-fees (accessed 8 August 2014).

Docherty T (2007) *The English Question, or Academic Freedoms*. Eastbourne: Sussex Academic Press.

Docherty T (2011) *For the University: Democracy and the Future of the Institution*. London: Bloomsbury Academic.

Docherty T (2011) The unseen academy. *Times Higher Education*, 10 November.

Eastwood D (2007) Goodbye to the RAE ... and hello to the REF. *Times Higher Education*, 30 November.

Eastwood D (2008) We can win the double. *Times Higher Education*, 29 May.

Foucault M (1995) *Discipline and Punish: The Birth of the Prison*. New York: Vintage.

Fox A (2002) The wrong result. *Guardian*, 17 July.

Garner R (2014) The academic fat cats: Vice-chancellors at Britain's top universities get £22,000 pay rises – as lecturers are stuck on 1 per cent. *The Independent*, 2 January.

Gill J (2008) Peer review must be at the heart of REF, expert says. *Times Higher Education*, 17 July.

Gill J (2009) Keep peer input in REF, urge panels. *Times Higher Education*, 8 January.

Ginsberg B (2011) *The Fall of the Faculty: The Rise of the All-Administrative University and Why It Matters*. New York: Oxford University Press.

Goldsmiths College, University of London (2013) An update on REF selections decisions from Professor Jane Powell. Available at: http://www.gold.ac.uk/staff-news/content/10july-ref/ (accessed 10 July 2013).

Graziosi B (2014) Sex and the REF. *Times Higher Education*, 20 March.

Grove J (2013) Higher Education Pay Survey, 2013. *Times Higher Education*, 28 March.

Halsall G (2013) Lancaster latest. In: Historian on the Edge, 15 October 2013. Available at: http://600transformer.blogspot.com/2013_10_01_archive.html (accessed 20 January 2014).

Harnad S (2008) Citations ideas 1. *Times Higher Education*, 4 January.

Harrison P (2014) The perils of REF 'irradiation'. *Times Higher Education*, 24 April.

Haynie D (2013) Universities with the largest financial endowments. *US News*, 1 October.

Higher Education Funding Council for England (HEFCE) (2003) Review of research assessment. Report by Sir Gareth Roberts to the UK funding bodies, May 2003. Available at: http://www.ra-review.ac.uk/reports/roberts/roberts_summary.pdf (accessed 12 August 2014).

Higher Education Funding Council for England (HEFCE) (2004) RAE2008: units of Assessment and Recruitment of Panel Members (July 2004). Available at: http://www.rae.ac.uk/pubs/2004/03/ (accessed 12 August 2014).

Higher Education Funding Council for England (HEFCE) (2009) RAE 2008 accountability review. PA Consulting Group, May 2009. Available at: http://www.hefce.ac.uk/pubs/rereports/year/2009/rae2008accountabilityreview/ (accessed 12 August 2014).

Higher Education Funding Council for England (HEFCE) (2010) Funding for universities and colleges in 2010-11. Circular Letter, February 2010. Available at: http://

www.hefce.ac.uk/pubs/year/2010/cl022010/name,62741,en.html (accessed 12 August 2014).

Higher Education Funding Council for England (HEFCE) (2010) REF2014: units of assessment and recruitment of expert panels. Available at: http://www.ref.ac.uk/pubs/2010-01/ (accessed 12 August 2014).

Higher Education Funding Council for England (HEFCE) (2011) REF2014: analysis of panel membership. Available at: http://www.ref.ac.uk/pubs/analysisofpanelmembership (accessed 12 August 2014).

Higher Education Funding Council for England (HEFCE) (2012) Funding for universities and colleges for 2012-13: Board decisions. Circular letter, 1 February 2014. Available at: http://www.hefce.ac.uk/pubs/ (accessed 12 August 2014).

Higher Education Funding Council for England (HEFCE) (2012) REF2014: assessment framework and guidance on submissions (updated to include addendum published in January 2012). Available at: http://www.ref.ac.uk/pubs/2011-02/ (accessed 12 August 2014).

Higher Education Funding Council for England (HEFCE) (2012) REF2014: nominating bodies. Available at: http://www.ref.ac.uk/panels/panelmembership/ (accessed 12 August 2014).

Higher Education Funding Council for England (HEFCE) (2012) REF2014: panel criteria and working methods. Available at: http://www.ref.ac.uk/pubs/2012-01/ (accessed 12 August 2014).

Higher Education Funding Council for England (HEFCE) (2012) REF Codes of Practice for the selection of staff: A report on good practice. Available at: http://www.ref.ac.uk/pubs/refcodesofpracticegoodpracticereport/#d.en.75885 (accessed 12 August 2014).

Higher Education Funding Council for England (HEFCE) (2013) How we fund research. Available at: http://www.hefce.ac.uk/whatwedo/rsrch/howfundr/ (accessed 12 August 2014).

Higher Education Funding Council for England (HEFCE) (2013) Main Panel D membership (December 2013). Available at: http://www.ref.ac.uk/panels/panelmembership/(accessed 12 August 2014).

Higher Education Funding Council for England (HEFCE) (2013) Mainstream QR funding. Available at: http://www.hefce.ac.uk/whatwedo/rsrch/howfundr/mainstreamqr/(accessed 12 August 2014).

Higher Education Funding Council for England (HEFCE) (2013) REF 2014: panel membership. Available at: http://www.ref.ac.uk/panels/panelmembership/ (accessed 12 August 2014).

Higher Education Funding Council for England (HEFCE) (2013) REF 2014: panel membership lists (updated December 2013). Available at: http://www.ref.ac.uk/panels/panelmembership/(accessed 12 August 2014).

Higher Education Funding Council for England (HEFCE) (2013) REF submissions received, 5 December 2013. Available at: http://www.hefce.ac.uk/news/newsarchive/2013/news85247.html (accessed 12 August 2014).

Higher Education Funding Council for England (HEFCE) (2014) Arrangements for the publication of results: REF 2014' (April 2014). Available at: http://www.ref.ac.uk/pubs/arrangementsforthepublicationofresults/ (accessed 25 June 2014).

Higher Education Funding Council for England (HEFCE) (2014) Funding for higher education in England for 2014-15: HEFCE grant letter from BIS, 10 February 2014. Available at: http://www.hefce.ac.uk/news/newsarchive/2014/name,85409,en. html (accessed 12 August 2014).

Higher Education Funding Council for England (HEFCE) (2014) More data on submissions to the REF (12 February 2014). Available at: http://www.hefce.ac.uk/news/newsarchive/2014/news85460.html (accessed 12 August 2014).

Higher Education Funding Council for England (HEFCE) (2014) Submissions (February 2014). Available at: http://www.ref.ac.uk/subguide/ (accessed 12 August 2014).

Higher Education Funding Council for England (HEFCE) (2014) REF2014: timetable. Available at: http://www.ref.ac.uk/timetable/ (accessed 12 August 2014).

Higher Education Funding Council for England (HEFCE) (nd) The QR funding formula. Available at: http://www.hefcw.ac.uk/documents/policy_areas/research/qr%20funding%20method.pdf (accessed 12 August 2014).

Higher Education Funding Council for England (HEFCE)/Universities UK (nd) Securing world-class research in UK universities: exploring the impact of block grant funding. Available at: http://www.universitiesuk.ac.uk/highereducation/Pages/WorldClassResearch.aspx#.U1VUm8bwDDE (accessed 12 August 2014).

Higher Education Statistics Agency (HESA) (2013) Staff in UK higher education. Available at: http://www.hesa.ac.uk/content/view/2694/393/ (accessed 29 January 2014).

Jump P (2012) Elite powers of concentration. *Times Higher Education,* 20 March.

Jump P (2012) Research intelligence – what's on the cards for the REF? *Times Higher Education,* 20 September.

Jump P. (2013) Cherry-pick submissions or risk picking up REF tab. *Times Higher Education,* 21 November.

Jump P (2013) Evolution of the REF. *Times Higher Education,* 17 October.

Jump P (2013) Paris post will not weaken panellist's 'duty' to REF. *Times Higher Education,* 28 March.

Jump P (2013) REF 'contextual data' decision could enrich league tables. *Times Higher Education,* 3 December.

Jump P (2013) REF non-submission may have consequences, Leicester warns. *Times Higher Education,* 8 August.

Jump P (2013) REF selectivity fears 'prove unfounded'. *Times Higher Education,* 5 December.

Jump P (2013) REF survey eases fears of selective game-playing. *Times Higher Education,* 17 January.

Jump P (2013) Staff submitted to REF likely to go above RAE total. *Times Higher Education,* 15 January.

Jump P (2013) Swansea's tough REF plans provoke disquiet. *Times Higher Education,* 5 September.

Jump P (2013) UCU uncovers high price of failure to hit REF targets. *Times Higher Education,* 3 October.

Jump P (2014) The REF: how was it for you? *Times Higher Education,* 27 February.

Kosch M (2012) In preparation for REF2014 – Mock REF and Units of Assessment. *SciTech Bulletin* #125 [nd (summer 2012)]. Available at: http://www.lancaster.ac.uk/sci-tech/bulletin/0125-2012-05-04.html (accessed 23 January 2014).

Kuhn TS (1962) *The Structure of Scientific Revolutions*. Chicago: Chicago University Press.

Lancaster University (2013) Examination of research degrees: guidance notes. Available at: http://www.lancaster.ac.uk/sbs/registry/docs/ExternalExaminers/ guidance-notes-research-degree.pdf (accessed 20 April 2014).

Lancaster University (2010) Performance and development review (PDR) policy. Available at: http://www.lancaster.ac.uk/hr/pdr/files/PDRPolicy.pdf (accessed 3 February 2014).

Lancaster University (2012) Promotion to readership and personal chair: procedures and criteria. Available at: http://www.lancaster.ac.uk/hr/total-reward/files/ccrcrit. html (accessed 3 January 2014).

Lancaster University (2012) REF 2014 Code of Practice. Available at: http://www.lancaster.ac.uk/depts/research/lancaster/REF2014.html (accessed 20 January 2014).

Lancaster University (2013) REF statement. Available at: http://www.lancaster.ac.uk/ depts/research/lancaster/REF2014.html (accessed 17 January 2014).

Lombardi JV (2010) In pursuit of Number ONE. In: Capaldi ED, Lombardi JV, Abbey CW and Craig DD (eds) *The Top American Universities: 2010 Annual Report*. Tempe: Arizona State University, Center for Measuring University Performance, 7.

Maitland FW (2001) *The Constitutional History of England*. New York: The Lawbook Exchange (reprint of 1908 edition).

Morgan J (2013) Bahram Bekhradnia: a critical friend delivers home truths. *Times Higher Education*, 11 April.

Morgan J (2013) Undergraduate numbers cap 'to be abolished' – Osborne. *Times Higher Education*, 5 December.

Morgan J (2014) 'Massive' budget hole predicted as RAB charge rises. *Times Higher Education*, 21 March.

National Association of College and University Business Officers and Commonfund Institute (2014) 2013 NACUBO-Commonfund Study of Endowments. Available at: http://www.nacubo.org/Documents/EndowmentFiles/2013NCSEPressRelease Final.pdf (accessed 15 April 2014).

National Endowment for the Humanities (NEH) (2012) NEH Grants. NEH's Application Review Process. Available at: http://www.neh.gov/grants/application-process#panel (accessed 11 August 2014).

New York University (2008) New York University Promotion and Tenure Guidelines. Available at: http://www.nyu.edu/about/policies-guidelines-compliance/ policies-and-guidelines/promotion-and-tenure-guidelines.html (accessed 28 December 2013).

Palladino P (2013) Why the REF is bad for the very idea of a university. UCU REFWatch, 10 December. Available at: http://ref.web.ucu.org.uk/2013/12/10/ why-the-ref-is-bad-for-the-very-idea-of-the-university/ (accessed 8 August 2014).

Quality Assurance Agency for Higher Education (QAA) (2013) Institutional review. Available at: http://www.qaa.ac.uk/InstitutionReports/types-of-review/IRENI/Pages/ default.aspx (accessed 8 March 2014).

QS World University Rankings (2013) Available at: http://www.topuniversities.com/ qs-world-university-rankings (accessed 11 February 2014).

QS World University Rankings (2013) Methodology. Available at: http://www. topuniversities.com/university-rankings-articles/world-university-rankings/ qs-world-university-rankings-methodology (accessed 11 February 2014).

Research Councils UK (RCUK) (2013) About the research councils. Available at: http://www.rcuk.ac.uk/about/Pages/home.aspx (accessed 5 January 2014).

Rohn J (2012) Business as usual in judging the worth of a researcher? *Guardian*, Occam's Corner, 30 November.

Russell Group of Universities (2013) Research at Russell Group Universities. Available at: http://www.russellgroup.ac.uk/research/ (accessed 12 February 2014).

Russell Group of Universities (2009) The concentration of research funding in the UK: driving excellence and competing globally (Autumn 2009). Available at: http://www.russellgroup.ac.uk/Policies-Research-funding/ (accessed 17 January 2014).

Sample I (2007) The God of small things. *Guardian*, 16 November.

Sarchet P (2013) REF procedures 'shambolic' at Warwick. Research Fortnight, 13 November. Available at: http://pennysarchet.wordpress.com (accessed 12 August 2014).

Sayer D (1990) *Capitalism and Modernity: An Excursus on Marx and Weber*. London: Routledge.

Sayer D (2013) Blog posts on the REF: The Kafkan world of the British 'Research Excellence Framework' (13 August 2013); Kafkarna continues: REF gloves off at Lancaster University (28 September 2013); Update from Wonderland: the Lancaster History REF farce goes on (5 October 2013); Lancaster's REF: Stockholm syndrome or worse? (10 October 2013); Getting nasty: Lancaster demands I censor my blogposts (16 October 2013); More REF: Warwick University Limited? (19 October 2013); Lancaster response to REF appeal: all is for the best in the best of all possible worlds (21 October 2013); Lancaster REF appeal: castle closed, reasons confidential (28 October 2013); GAG (1 November 2013); REF: tears of rage, tears of grief (4 November 2013); A mildly annoying bit of bureaucracy? Time to think long, hard and deep about the legacy of REF 2014 (8 November 2013); Getting nastier: Lancaster REF – the victimization starts (20 November 2013); REF deadline day – all together now! (29 November 2013); The odious machine (3 December 2013). Available at: http://coastsofbohemia.com (all accessed 11 August 2014).

Scott P (2013) Why research assessment is out of control. *Guardian*, 4 November.

Social Sciences and Humanities Research Council (Canada) (SSHRC) (2013) Merit review. Available at: http://www.sshrc-crsh.gc.ca/funding-financement/merit_review-evaluation_du_merite/index-eng.aspx (accessed 18 January 2014).

Social Sciences and Humanities Research Council (Canada) (SSHRC) (2013) Principles for merit review. Available at: http://www.sshrc-crsh.gc.ca/funding-financement/merit_review-evaluation_du_merite/index-eng.aspx (accessed 18 January 2014).

Social Sciences and Humanities Research Council (Canada) (SSHRC) (2013) SSHRC manual for adjudication committee members 2013-14. Available at: http://www.sshrc-crsh.gc.ca/funding-financement/merit_review-evaluation_du_merite/adjudication_manual_2013-guide_members_2013-eng.pdf (accessed 18 January 2014).

Thompson EP (1965) The peculiarities of the English. In: *The Socialist Register 1965*. London: Merlin, 311-362. Available at: https://www.marxists.org/archive/thompson-ep/1965/english.htm (accessed 12 August 2014).

Times Higher Education (2013) World University Rankings 2013-2014. Available at: http://www.timeshighereducation.co.uk/world-university-rankings/2013-14/world-ranking (accessed 11 February 2014).

Times Higher Education (2013) World University Rankings 2013-14 methodology. Available at: http://www.timeshighereducation.co.uk/world-university-rankings/2013-14/world-ranking/methodology (accessed 11 February 2014).

Times Higher Education (2013) Rankings methodology: experts recognise these as the best. Available at: http://www.timeshighereducation.co.uk/world-university-rankings/2013/reputation-ranking/methodology (accessed 14 February 2014).

University of Birmingham (2013) Vice-Chancellor's profile. Available at: http://www.birmingham.ac.uk/university/welcome/vcprofile.aspx (accessed 22 February 2014).

University and College Union (UCU) (2013) About UCU. Available at: http://www.ucu.org.uk/1685 (accessed 16 April 2014).

University and College Union (UCU) (2007) National pay bargaining essential for equitable sector, says UCU. Available at: http://www.ucu.org.uk/index.cfm?articleid=2671#2100 (accessed 16 April 2007).

University and College Union (UCU) Warwick University branch. (2013) Warwick survey shows REF rules being bypassed and selection guidelines ignored. Available at: https://www.warwickucu.org.uk/sites/default/files/Warwick%20REF%20survey.pdf (accessed 11 August 2014).

University of Oregon, History Department (2013) Promotion and tenure policies: History department. Available at: http://academicaffairs.uoregon.edu/sites/default/files/HISTORY%20Promotion%20and%20Tenure%20Guidelines%202011.pdf (accessed 5 January 2014).

University of Oregon, Office of Academic Affairs (2013) Evaluation and promotion – tenure track. Available at: http://academicaffairs.uoregon.edu/evaluation-and-promotion-tenure-track (accessed 21 April 2014).

University of York (2013) Promotion of academic, research and teaching staff: procedures and criteria 2013-14. Available at: http://www.york.ac.uk/media/abouttheuniversity/supportservices/registrar-secretary/promotions/ProceduresCriteria2013-14.pdf (accessed 3 February 2014).

Voeten E (2013) Kansas Board of Regents restricts free speech for academics. *Washington Post*, The Monkey Cage blog, 19 December.

INDEX